Report to the Chairman, Subcommittee on the Middle East and North Africa, Committee on Foreign Affairs, House of Representatives

February 2014

COUNTERING OVERSEAS THREATS

I0448470

DOD and State Need to Address Gaps in Monitoring of Security Equipment Transferred to Lebanon

GAO Highlights

Highlights of GAO-14-161, a report to the Chairman, Subcommittee on the Middle East and North Africa, Committee on Foreign Affairs, House of Representatives

COUNTERING OVERSEAS THREATS

DOD and State Need to Address Gaps in Monitoring of Security Equipment Transferred to Lebanon

Why GAO Did This Study

Since 2009, the United States has allocated $671 million in security-related assistance for Lebanon to train, modernize, and equip the Lebanese Armed Forces and Internal Security Forces. The U.S. government established end-use monitoring programs to ensure that defense equipment is safeguarded. The Foreign Assistance Act prohibits certain assistance to any unit of foreign security forces if the Secretary of State has credible information that such a unit has committed a gross violation of human rights. GAO was asked to examine U.S. security-related assistance for Lebanon.

This report assesses the extent to which the U.S. government (1) disbursed or committed funds allocated for Lebanese security forces in fiscal years 2009 through 2013, (2) implemented end-use monitoring for equipment transferred to Lebanese security forces, and (3) vetted Lebanese recipients of U.S. security-related training for human rights violations. To address these objectives, GAO reviewed laws and regulations, analyzed agency data, and interviewed officials in Washington, D.C., and Beirut, Lebanon.

What GAO Recommends

GAO recommends that DOD ensure U.S. officials use required checklists to confirm Lebanese facilities' compliance with required safeguards, and that State maintain proper documentation of end-use checks and establish formal procedures to ensure that bureaus identify defense articles and any recommended physical security safeguards for storing them. DOD and State concurred.

View GAO-14-161. For more information, contact Charles Michael Johnson, Jr., at (202) 512-7331 or johnsoncm@gao.gov.

What GAO Found

The United States allocated $671 million for Lebanese security forces from fiscal year 2009 through fiscal year 2013. Of these total allocated funds, $477 million, or 71 percent, had been disbursed or committed by the end of fiscal year 2013. Nearly all of the allocations made in fiscal years 2009 through 2011 had been disbursed or committed. For the largest program, Foreign Military Financing, the Department of Defense (DOD) had committed about $352 million of the $481 million allocated in fiscal years 2009 through 2013.

Consistent with end-use monitoring requirements, DOD and the Department of State (State) conduct annual inventories for equipment transferred to Lebanese security forces. However, GAO found gaps in efforts to document and monitor physical security of some U.S. equipment transferred to Lebanese security forces that may weaken efforts to safeguard physical security of some equipment. First, while DOD annually inventories sensitive equipment by serial number, as required by its policy, U.S embassy officials in Beirut have not always used DOD's required checklists to document compliance with physical security safeguards. Second, State did not fully document 4 of the 10 end-use monitoring checks it conducted in fiscal years 2011 and 2012 for defense equipment the Lebanese government purchased commercially. State end-use monitoring guidance requires that specific information be documented and maintained for all such checks. Third, while State conducts an annual inventory of the equipment it transfers to the Lebanese security forces, State may not be ensuring that the recipients of defense articles implement recommended physical security safeguards because State lacks procedures to identify defense articles and any recommended safeguards for storing them.

Examples of Items Subject to End-Use Monitoring in Lebanon

Night vision device | Vehicles | Rifles

Source: GAO (photos).

GAO estimates that State vetted 100 percent of the Lebanese students that attended U.S.-funded security-related training from October 10, 2010, through April 30, 2013, for human rights violations. On the basis of a cross-check analysis of vetting data and a sample of names from six training rosters, GAO estimates that State vetted all of the 7,104 Lebanese students that attended training during that period.

_____ United States Government Accountability Office

Contents

Tables

Figures

Abbreviations

DOD	Department of Defense
DSCA	Defense Security Cooperation Agency
FMS	Foreign Military Sales
INCLE	International Narcotics Control and Law Enforcement
INL	Bureau of International Narcotics Control and Law Enforcement Affairs
INVEST	International Vetting and Security Tracking database
ISF	Internal Security Forces
LAF	Lebanese Armed Forces
NADR	Nonproliferation, Antiterrorism, Demining, and Related programs
State	Department of State

February 26, 2014

The Honorable Ileana Ros-Lehtinen
Chairman
Subcommittee on the Middle East and North Africa
Committee on Foreign Affairs
House of Representatives

Dear Madam Chairman:

Lebanon is a religiously diverse country transitioning toward independence and democratic consolidation after a 15-year civil war and subsequent occupation by Syrian and Israeli forces. Following Syrian withdrawal from Lebanon in 2005 and the war between Israel and the Lebanese militant group Hezbollah in the summer of 2006, the United States significantly increased security-related assistance for Lebanon to support its efforts to build a stable, secure, and independent democracy. U.S. agencies have allocated over $925 million in security-related assistance for Lebanon from fiscal years 2007 through 2012,[1] to train, modernize, and equip the Lebanese Armed Forces (LAF) and Internal Security Forces (ISF). Those efforts and the U.S. investment are now challenged by new tensions resulting from spillover of the civil war in Syria. Members of Congress have raised concerns about U.S. assistance to Lebanon and possible weapons smuggling to Hezbollah and other armed groups, given Hezbollah's involvement in the Lebanese government and a clash between the LAF and Israeli Defense Forces along Lebanon's and Israel's shared border.

---

[1]According to officials from the Departments of Defense and State, there is no consensus about whether some funding accounts that support security cooperation or security sector reform should be labeled "assistance." For the purposes of this report, we consider accounts that funded overt security-related activities in Lebanon to be security-related assistance.

This is the second of two reports responding to your request that we review U.S. security equipment and training for Lebanon.[2] In this report, we assess the extent to which the U.S. government (1) disbursed or committed funds allocated for Lebanese security forces in fiscal years 2009 through 2013, (2) implemented end-use monitoring for equipment transferred to Lebanese security forces, and (3) vetted Lebanese recipients of U.S. security-related training for human rights violations.

To address these objectives, we obtained funding data from the Department of Defense (DOD) and the Department of State (State) on programs that provide security-related assistance to Lebanon. We also examined documents from DOD and State, such as cables, handbooks, and compliance and inventory reports, and analyzed data on U.S.-provided equipment, training, end-use checks, and human rights vetting of applicants for security-related equipment and training. To assess the extent to which DOD and State complied with their regulations and guidance on end-use monitoring and human rights vetting, we selected and analyzed the following: a nongeneralizable random sample of 30 items out of 184 provided to the LAF at two locations in Beirut that required enhanced end-use monitoring for physical inspection; a judgmental sample of all 10 end-use checks performed by State for equipment exported to Lebanon in fiscal years 2010 through 2012; and a generalizable random sample of 118 of 7,104 Lebanese students who were vetted for human rights violations from October 10, 2010, through April 30, 2013. We interviewed DOD and State officials in Washington, D.C.; at the U.S. Central Command in Tampa, Florida; and at the U.S. Embassy in Beirut, Lebanon. We also interviewed officials of the LAF and ISF in Lebanon. To assess the reliability of the data provided, we requested and reviewed information from officials from each agency regarding the agency's underlying financial data systems and the checks, controls, and reviews used to ensure the accuracy and reliability of the data provided. We determined that the data provided were sufficiently reliable for the purposes of this report. Appendix I provides a detailed description of our scope and methodology.

---

[2]In the first report, we assessed the extent to which the U.S. government adjusted its strategic goals and security assistance programs in Lebanon, funded assistance programs for Lebanese security forces, and evaluated the effectiveness of security assistance programs in Lebanon from fiscal years 2007 through 2012. See GAO, *Security Assistance to Lebanon: Evaluations Needed to Determine Effectiveness of U.S. Aid to Lebanon's Security Forces*, GAO-13-289 (Washington, D.C.: Mar. 19, 2013).

We conducted this performance audit from April 2013 to February 2014 in accordance with generally accepted government auditing standards. Those standards require that we plan and perform the audit to obtain sufficient, appropriate evidence to provide a reasonable basis for our findings and conclusions based on our audit objectives. We believe that the evidence obtained provides a reasonable basis for our findings and conclusions based on our audit objectives.

Background

Lebanon is a small, religiously diverse country on the Mediterranean Sea that borders Israel and Syria (see fig. 1).

Figure 1: Map of Lebanon

Source: GAO; United Nations 2010 and Map Resources (maps).

Religious tensions among Lebanon's Maronite Christians, Sunni Muslims, and Shiite Muslims, and others, along with an influx of Palestinian refugees, for decades have underpinned Lebanon's internal conflicts as well as its conflicts with neighboring countries. Hezbollah emerged in Lebanon as a powerful Islamic militant group and since 2005, a member of Hezbollah has held a cabinet position in the Lebanese government. Hezbollah is funded by Iran and has been designated by the United States and Israel as a terrorist organization. In the summer of 2006, Hezbollah and Israel entered into a month-long conflict that ended with the adoption of United Nations Resolution 1701 by both the Israeli and

Lebanese governments.[3] The resolution called for, among other things, Israeli withdrawal from southern Lebanon in parallel with the deployment of Lebanese and United Nations forces and the disarmament of all armed groups in Lebanon. Instability arising from the civil war in neighboring Syria that began in 2011 has exacerbated sectarian conflict within Lebanon. In May 2013, Hezbollah leaders confirmed their intervention in the Syrian conflict. Figure 2 presents a timeline of selected political events in Lebanon.

Figure 2: Timeline of Selected Political Events in Lebanon, from October 1990 to September 2013

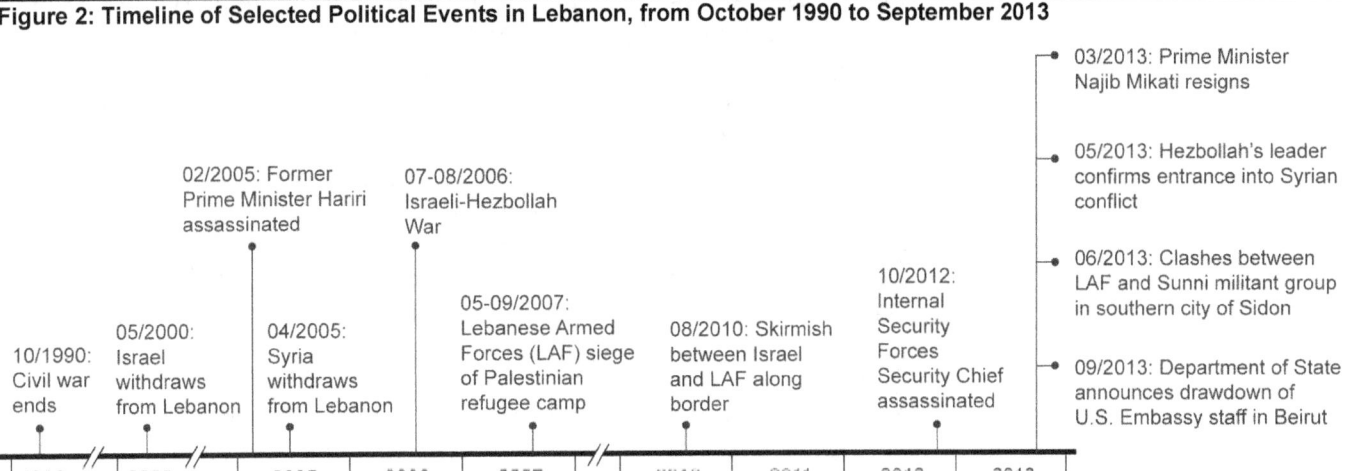

Source: GAO analysis of public information

Since the end of the 2006 Israeli-Hezbollah war, the United States has kept strategic goals for Lebanon constant. These goals are to support Lebanon as a stable, secure, and independent democracy. The overarching priorities of U.S. assistance programs for Lebanon focus on supporting Lebanese sovereignty and stability and countering the influence of Syria and Iran. Security-related goals for Lebanon focus on counterterrorism and regional stability or internal security, and corresponding activities seek to support development of the LAF and the ISF as the only legitimate providers of Lebanon's security. The United States has provided security equipment and training to the LAF, which is generally responsible for providing border security, counterterrorism, and

[3]S.C. Res. 1701, U.N. Doc. S/Res/1701 (2006).

GAO-14-161 Security-Related Assistance to Lebanon

national defense, and to the ISF, or national police force, which is generally responsible for maintaining law and order in Lebanon.

End-Use Monitoring

In 1996, Congress amended the Arms Export Control Act of 1976, which authorizes the President to control the sale or export of defense articles and services,[4] to require the President to establish a program for monitoring the end-use of defense articles[5] and defense services sold, leased, or exported under the act, including through Foreign Military Sales (FMS) and direct commercial sales,[6] or the Foreign Assistance Act of 1961.[7] The amendment specified that the program should provide reasonable assurances that recipients comply with restrictions imposed by the U.S. government on the use, transfer, and security of defense articles and defense services.[8] The President delegated responsibilities for the program to the Secretary of Defense, insofar as they relate to defense articles and defense services sold, leased, or transferred under FMS, and to the Secretary of State, insofar as they relate to commercial exports licensed under the Arms Export Control Act.[9] For FMS, DOD's Defense Security Cooperation Agency (DSCA) is responsible for end-use monitoring; for direct commercial sales, State's Directorate of Defense Trade Controls is responsible for end-use monitoring. In addition to the end-use monitoring requirements under the Arms Export Control Act, the Foreign Assistance Act, as amended, directs the President to take all reasonable steps to ensure that aircraft and other equipment made available to foreign countries for international narcotics control under the Foreign Assistance Act are used only in ways that are consistent with the

[4]Arms Export Control Act, as amended, 22 U.S.C. §§ 2751 et seq.

[5]Throughout this report, we use the terms "equipment" and "security equipment" synonymously with "defense articles."

[6]The FMS program allows recipient countries to obtain defense articles from U.S. military departments. Direct commercial sales involve purchases directly from U.S. companies.

[7]22 U.S.C. § 2785.

[8]22 U.S.C. § 2785(a).

[9]See Executive Order 13637, § 1(p), 78 Fed. Reg. 16130, Mar. 8, 2013, set out as a note under 22 U.S.C. § 2751. Functions were previously delegated by Executive Order 11958, which was formerly set out as a note under 22 U.S.C. § 2751 and was revoked, subject to a savings provision, by section 4 of Executive Order 13637.

purposes for which such equipment was made available.[10] State's Bureau of International Narcotics Control and Law Enforcement Affairs (INL) has implemented this requirement by means of its End-Use Monitoring Program.

DOD and State Leahy Laws

To help ensure that U.S. assistance is not used to support human rights violators, Congress prohibits certain types of assistance from being provided to foreign security forces implicated in human rights abuses. Section 620M of the Foreign Assistance Act prohibits the United States from providing assistance under the Foreign Assistance Act or the Arms Export Control Act to any unit of a foreign country's security forces if the Secretary of State has credible information that such unit has committed a gross violation of human rights.[11] This provision is known colloquially as the State Leahy law. DOD's annual appropriation contains a similar provision, known colloquially as the DOD Leahy law. The current version prohibits funds from being used to support training, equipment, or other assistance for security forces of a foreign country if the Secretary of Defense has received credible information that the unit has committed a gross violation of human rights.[12] DOD, in consultation with State, must give full consideration to any credible information available to State relating to human rights violations by a unit of the foreign security forces before it conducts training for the unit. According to State, Leahy laws and the corresponding policies developed to enforce and supplement these laws are intended to leverage U.S. assistance to encourage foreign governments to prevent their security forces from committing human rights violations and to hold their forces accountable when violations

---

[10]Section 484 of the Foreign Assistance Act, Pub. L. No. 87-195, codified as amended at 22 U.S.C. § 2291c(b).

[11]22 U.S.C. § 2378d.

[12]For the purposes of this report, we use the term "Leahy laws" to refer collectively to the prohibition on assistance to security forces in section 620M of the Foreign Assistance Act of 1961 and the similar recurring provision in the DOD appropriations act prohibiting funding for training, equipment, or other assistance involving units of security forces, which was most recently enacted in section 8057 of the Consolidated Appropriations Act, 2014. Pub. L. No. 113-76, § 8057, 128 Stat. 5, 118-119. We refer to the Foreign Assistance Act provision as the "State Leahy law" and the DOD appropriations provision as the "DOD Leahy law." DOD and State use the term "Leahy laws" for these requirements, introduced in legislation by Senator Leahy, in order to distinguish them from other human rights requirements.

occur.[13] According to State, U.S. programs subject to the Leahy laws in Lebanon include Foreign Military Financing; International Narcotics Control and Law Enforcement (INCLE); Nonproliferation, Antiterrorism, Demining, and Related programs; and Sections 1206 and 1207 authorities. See appendix II for additional information on the U.S. human rights vetting process.

U.S. Agencies Have Disbursed or Committed Most of the $671 Million Allocated for Security-Related Assistance Programs for Lebanon in Fiscal Years 2009 through 2013

The United States allocated $671 million for security-related assistance for Lebanon from fiscal year 2009 through fiscal year 2013. Of these total allocated funds, $477 million, or 71 percent, had been disbursed or committed by the end of fiscal year 2013. Nearly all of the allocations made in fiscal years 2009 through 2011 had been disbursed or committed.

Since 2007, the United States has provided security-related assistance for Lebanon through the Foreign Military Financing program; the International Military Education and Training program; the INCLE program; the Nonproliferation, Antiterrorism, Demining, and Related programs;[14] and Section 1206 and 1207 authorities for training and equipping foreign militaries and security forces and for reconstruction, stabilization, and security activities in foreign countries, respectively. For the largest program, Foreign Military Financing, DOD had committed about $352 million of the $481 million allocated from fiscal years 2009 through 2013. Table 1 presents the amounts of funds allocated, committed, or disbursed to these programs for Lebanon in fiscal years 2009 through 2013. Appendix III provides additional information on the status of these funds.

---

[13]See GAO, *Human Rights: Additional Guidance, Monitoring, and Training Could Improve Implementation of the Leahy Laws,* GAO-13-866 (Washington, D.C.: Sept. 25, 2013).

[14]The Department of State's Nonproliferation, Antiterrorism, Demining, and Related programs provide security-related assistance for Lebanon through three subaccounts: Antiterrorism Assistance, Counterterrorism Financing, and Export Control and Related Border Security.

GAO-14-161 Security-Related Assistance to Lebanon

Table 1: Funds Allocated and Funds Committed or Disbursed by U.S. Security-Related Assistance Programs for Lebanese Security Forces, Fiscal Years (FY) 2009-2013

Dollars in thousands

Program or account	FY2009	FY2010	FY2011	FY2012	FY2013	Total
Foreign Military Financing						
Allocated	159,700	100,000	74,850	75,000	71,207	**480,757**
Committed	159,700	100,000	74,850	17,629	0	**352,179**
International Military Education and Training						
Allocated	2,278	2,500	2,467	2,372	2,850	**12,467**
Disbursed	1,992	2,216	2,130	1,868	943	**9,149**
International Narcotics Control and Law Enforcement						
Allocated	6,000	20,000	19,500	24,000	15,406	**84,906**
Disbursed	5,938	15,781	6,551	486	453	**29,209**
NADR[a] - Antiterrorism Assistance						
Allocated	3,714	4,600	2,000	2,000	1,994	**14,312**
Disbursed	2,940	3,953	1,464	1,464	0	**9,821**
NADR - Counterterrorism Financing						
Allocated	0	0	174	0	0	**618**
Disbursed	0	0	2	0	0	**603**
NADR - Export Control and Related Border Security						
Allocated	400	800	800	1,050	800	**3,850**
Disbursed	400	798	553	467	0	**2,218**
Section 1206						
Allocated	49,240	16,582	0	0	8,700	**74,522**
Disbursed	49,240	16,582	0	0	8,700	**74,522**
Section 1207[b]						
Allocated	508	0	0	0	0	**508**
Disbursed	0	0	0	0	0	**0**
Total allocated	**221,840**	**144,486**	**99,791**	**104,422**	**100,957**	**671,496**
Total disbursed or committed	**220,210**	**139,330**	**85,550**	**21,914**	**10,096**	**477,100**

Source: GAO analysis of State and DOD data.

Notes: Data are as of September 30, 2013. Agencies may have several years in which to obligate and disburse or commit allocated funds. App. III provides additional detailed information on the amount of unobligated balances and unliquidated obligations for each funding account.

[a]Nonproliferation, Antiterrorism, Demining, and Related (NADR) programs. The Department of State's NADR security-related assistance for Lebanon has been provided through three subaccounts: Antiterrorism Assistance, Counterterrorism Financing, and Export Control and Related Border Security.

[b]Section 1207 authority expired on September 30, 2010.

Table 2 describes the U.S. security-related assistance programs for Lebanon and their goals, and identifies the agencies that implement them.

Table 2: U.S. Security-Related Assistance Programs for Lebanon

Program and implementing agency	Description	Program goals as stated by agency officials
Foreign Military Financing[a] Department of Defense (DOD)	Provides grants and loans to foreign governments for the acquisition of U.S. defense equipment, services, and training.	To bolster the capability of the Lebanese Armed Forces (LAF), nurture the bilateral military relationship between the United States and the LAF, and continue encouraging establishment of a stable, legal, and pro-U.S. civil government.
International Military Education and Training DOD	Provides training, such as technical and professional military education, on a grant basis to students from allied and friendly nations.	To bolster the capability of the LAF, nurture the bilateral military relationship between the United States and the LAF, and continue encouraging establishment of a stable, legal, and pro-U.S. civil government.
International Narcotics Control and Law Enforcement Department of State (State)	Supports country and global programs critical to combating transnational crime and illicit threats, including efforts against terrorist networks in the illegal drug trade and illicit enterprises.	To (1) build Lebanon's operational capacity to combat crime and prevent and respond to terror attacks, and (2) assist Lebanon in developing the Internal Security Forces (ISF) into a competent, professional, and democratic police force with the necessary training, equipment, and institutional capacity to enforce the rule of law in Lebanon, cement sovereign Lebanese government control over its territory, and protect the Lebanese people.
NADR[b] - Antiterrorism Assistance State	Trains civilian security and law enforcement personnel from friendly governments in police procedures that deal with terrorism.	To develop and build the Lebanese government's capacities in border security, mid- and senior-level leadership development, and counterterrorism investigations.
NADR - Counterterrorism Financing State	Provides training for law enforcement officials, prosecutors, and judges, among others, in specific elements of money laundering and terrorist financing crimes.	To deny terrorists access to money, resources, and support.
NADR - Export Control and Related Border Security State	Assesses countries' export control systems and provides a variety of assistance to help countries develop and improve their strategic trade and related border control systems.	To strengthen the capability of Lebanese enforcement agencies to effectively control cross-border trade in strategic goods.
Section 1206 authority DOD and State	Trains and equips foreign military and nonmilitary maritime forces to conduct counterterrorist operations or support military and stability operations in which the U.S. armed services are a participant.	To bolster the capability of the LAF, nurture the bilateral military relationship between the United States and the LAF, and continue encouraging establishment of a stable, legal, and pro-U.S. civil government.

Program and implementing agency	Description	Program goals as stated by agency officials
Section 1207 authority[c] State	Provides for reconstruction, stabilization, and security activities in foreign countries.	To strengthen Lebanon's internal security forces after armed conflicts in 2006 and 2007.

Source: GAO analysis of State and DOD information.

Notes: Some of the information on goals is derived from discussions with DOD and State officials.

[a]Foreign Military Financing can fund the transfer of services or equipment through either Direct Commercial Sales or Foreign Military Sales.

[b]Nonproliferation, Antiterrorism, Demining, and Related (NADR) programs. The Department of State's NADR security-related assistance for Lebanon has been provided through three programs: Antiterrorism Assistance, Counterterrorism Financing, and Export Control and Related Border Security.

[c]Section 1207 authority expired on September 30, 2010.

We provide examples of the types of equipment some of these programs provide to the Lebanese security forces in the next section.

DOD and State Monitor End Use of Equipment Transferred to Lebanese Security Forces, but Gaps in Documentation and Security Checks May Limit Efforts to Safeguard Some Equipment

DOD and State conduct end-use monitoring for equipment each has provided or authorized for sale to Lebanese security forces, but gaps in implementation of procedures may limit efforts to safeguard some equipment. DOD annually inventories sensitive equipment by serial number, as required by its policy; however, U.S. embassy officials in Beirut have not always used DOD's required checklists to document compliance with security safeguards and accountability procedures. In addition, State officials in headquarters and at the U.S. Embassy in Beirut did not always document the results of end-use monitoring checks as specified in State guidance. Finally, State INL officials annually inventory all equipment INL has provided to the ISF, but INL may not be ensuring that the ISF is implementing recommended physical security safeguards for defense articles because INL lacks procedures to identify defense articles and the recommended safeguards for storing them.

DOD Officials Conduct Annual Inventories in End-Use Monitoring for Sensitive Equipment

DOD officials conduct annual inventories as part of end-use monitoring through the Golden Sentry program, which is DOD's program to comply with requirements of the Arms Export Control Act, as amended, related to the end use of defense articles and services. DOD personnel at U.S. missions worldwide conduct the monitoring activities established and overseen by DSCA.[15] Under this program, DOD conducts two levels of monitoring: routine end-use monitoring and enhanced end-use monitoring.

- Routine end-use monitoring: DOD conducts routine end-use monitoring for defense articles and services sold through FMS that do not have any unique conditions associated with their transfer. Routine end-use monitoring is conducted in conjunction with other required security-related duties. For example, U.S. officials might observe how a host country's military is using U.S. equipment when visiting a military installation on other business.
- Enhanced end-use monitoring: DOD conducts enhanced end-use monitoring for defense services, technologies, or articles specifically identified as sensitive—such as night vision devices. DOD policy requires serial number inventories for defense articles requiring enhanced end-use monitoring following delivery of the articles and at regular intervals thereafter. In addition, Letters of Offer and Acceptance, the FMS purchase agreements authorizing the sale of an item, may contain specialized notes or provisos requiring the purchaser to adhere to certain physical security and accountability requirements.[16]

With respect to enhanced end-use monitoring, DSCA's policy manual for end-use monitoring, the Security Assistance Management Manual,[17] and

---

[15]DSCA is the central agency that coordinates global security cooperation programs, funding, and efforts across the Office of the Secretary of Defense, Joint Staff, State Department, combatant commands, the military services, and U.S. industry. DSCA administers the Golden Sentry program. Activities include conducting regional forums to provide updated policy guidance, visiting DOD overseas officials to assess their compliance with Golden Sentry policy, and publishing and disseminating end-use monitoring best practices and lessons learned.

[16]Letters of Offer and Acceptance are FMS purchase agreements between the United States and a foreign purchaser. The specialized notes that may be in these agreements are outlined in Chapter 5 of the *Security Assistance Management Manual.*

[17]Department of Defense, Defense Security Cooperation Agency, *Security Assistance Management Manual,* (Washington, D.C.: Apr. 30, 2012), accessed January 9, 2014, http://www.samm.dsca.mil/.

the associated standard operating procedures for Beirut require DOD officials annually to

- conduct a physical inventory of 100 percent of designated defense articles,[18]
- conduct physical security checks of facilities where the equipment is kept, and
- use and maintain records of equipment-specific checklists that outline the physical security requirements for Lebanese facilities that store the equipment.

Officials of DOD's Office of Defense Cooperation in Beirut[19] told us that they annually conduct an inventory involving the inspection of serial numbers for 100 percent of defense articles requiring enhanced end-use monitoring. Such equipment includes certain types of missiles, night vision devices, sniper rifles, aircraft, and unmanned aerial vehicles. Figure 3 shows examples of defense articles provided to the LAF.[20]

---

[18]According to the DSCA *Security Assistance Management Manual*, enhanced end-use monitoring is conducted through planned and coordinated visits to the host nation's installations and verification of in-country receipt of defense articles by serial number within 90 days of delivery. Subsequent inventories require serial number verification, physical security checks of storage sites or other facilities where defense articles designated for enhanced end-use monitoring are located, and verification that recipients are complying with the terms and conditions stated in the transfer agreements.

[19]The Office of Defense Cooperation executes security assistance and cooperation programs in partnership with U.S. Embassy country teams and under the direction of the U.S. ambassador.

[20]According to a DOD official in Beirut, DOD officials also conduct 100 percent annual inventories for other items provided to Lebanon that are not subject to enhanced end-use monitoring, although this is not a requirement of DSCA's *Security Assistance Management Manual*.

Figure 3: Photographs of Lebanese Armed Forces Equipment Prepared for End-Use Monitoring

Night vision devices

Rifles

Source: GAO.

During our visit to Beirut in July 2013, we determined that DOD and the LAF accounted for almost 100 percent of the defense items in our sample in two locations. To assess the extent to which DOD accounts for equipment provided to the LAF, we drew a random sample by serial number from DOD's equipment inventory database for two locations we planned to visit during our fieldwork in Lebanon.[21] The items in the sample included various types of night vision devices at one location and various types of night vision devices and a sniper rifle at the other location. Although the results cannot be generalized to these or other locations, they showed that DOD and the LAF accounted for almost 100 percent of the items in our sample in both locations. In addition, during our visit, DOD performed its 2013 inventory of 100 percent of the equipment provided to one of the LAF regiments, including some new equipment not previously inventoried. The DOD officials were able to confirm that all equipment was either physically present or accounted for through documentation. Figure 4 shows U.S. officials conducting the inventory of U.S.-provided equipment at an LAF facility.

Figure 4: U.S. Officials Conducting an Inventory of U.S.-Provided Equipment at a Lebanese Armed Forces Facility

Source: GAO.

---

[21]The sample consisted of 15 items from each location, from a total of 68 items at one location and 116 items at the other. We directly observed 13 of the 15 items at one location and 9 of the 15 at the other location. DOD and LAF officials showed us documentation that accounted for the whereabouts of the items we were not able to inspect. For example, the LAF presented documents showing that some items were signed out to another LAF location. In such cases, DOD officials in Beirut require the LAF to present equipment for inspection at a later date.

When U.S. travel restrictions due to security concerns prohibit U.S. embassy personnel from traveling to specific areas of Lebanon in which some LAF storage facilities are located, DOD officials in Beirut require the LAF to bring the equipment to a central location in Beirut to allow the DOD officials to conduct the annual inventory. DOD quarterly reports from 2011 through 2013 show 100 percent accountability for equipment provided to the LAF.

DOD Officials Have Not Always Used Required Checklists to Document Compliance with Security Safeguards

As part of end-use monitoring, DSCA's Security Assistance Management Manual and the standard operating procedures for Beirut require DOD officials to conduct physical security checks of LAF facilities, using a required checklist to document accountability and physical security of U.S.-provided equipment.[22] While DOD's quarterly reports from 2011 through 2013 show 100 percent accountability for equipment provided to the LAF, during our site visit in July 2013, we determined that DOD officials in Beirut were not using the required checklist to document compliance with physical security safeguards. The DOD manual specifically directs that enhanced end-use monitoring must be performed using checklists developed by the military departments. Furthermore, according to the manual, all such checks must be recorded, with the physical security and accountability checklists attached to the inventory records that must be maintained for 5 years.

According to a DOD official in Beirut, at least 75 percent of the U.S.-provided equipment subject to end-use monitoring is held in locations where DOD can and has conducted inspections to verify compliance with physical security requirements. For the remaining facilities, DOD mitigates security challenges by other means. DOD officials stated that a U.S. embassy employee who is a Lebanese national had visited some locations that U.S. officials were not able to visit because of security concerns and had conducted physical security compliance checks at those locations. For each of the remaining facilities that neither a U.S. official nor this Lebanese employee could personally inspect, DOD also requires the LAF to submit a letter attesting that the appropriate physical security measures had been implemented.

---

[22]Such physical security conditions might include fencing, a locked or guarded building structure, and specific types of doors and locks.

During our site visit in July 2013, we determined that when DOD officials in Beirut were able to conduct physical security checks, they were not using checklists for enhanced end-use monitoring required by DSCA's Security Assistance Management Manual to ensure that security safeguards and accountability procedures are in place. The manual directs that enhanced end-use monitoring must be performed using checklists developed by the military departments. Furthermore, according to the manual, all such checks must be recorded, with the physical security and accountability checklists attached to the inventory records that must be maintained for 5 years.

Our finding was consistent with the results of a 2011 DSCA compliance assessment visit, when DSCA officials also found that the DOD Office of Defense Cooperation in Beirut was not using the required checklists to verify Lebanese compliance with facility security requirements.[23] In April 2012, U.S. officials in Beirut responded to the DSCA finding, stating that they planned to use the checklists during their 2012 annual inventory. In their response, they also stated that the requirement to use DSCA-provided checklists during inventories was captured in the post's updated standard operating procedures for end-use monitoring.[24] We followed up on this matter in September 2013 and found that, when presented examples of the checklists, DOD officials in Beirut said that they were not aware of the checklists. The officials, however, noted that the information requested in the checklists is the same type of information they enter into the Security Cooperation Information Portal, which is the system used to record end-use monitoring activities.[25] However, the documentation of the

---

[23]In 2011, DSCA conducted a compliance assessment visit to Lebanon that included a review of selected LAF facilities for compliance with requirements to safeguard U.S.-provided equipment. DSCA officials found that some LAF facilities did not meet certain safeguard requirements and recommended corrective actions. U.S. officials from the embassy inspected the facilities during the 2012 annual equipment inventory. According to the 2012 report on the results of that inventory, the LAF had upgraded doors and storage containers at facilities storing night vision devices, installed double barriers, moved some equipment to more secure facilities, and equipped some facilities with external lighting.

[24]Office of Defense Cooperation, U.S. Embassy, Beirut, *End-Use Monitoring Program: Golden Sentry Program End-Use Monitoring and Enhanced End-Use Monitoring* (Beirut, Lebanon: April 25, 2012).

[25]The Security Cooperation Information Portal is a web-based database DOD designed to manage various security assistance activities, including the Golden Sentry program. It includes information on the defense articles purchased by each country, the date that these items were last inventoried, and the status of their inventories.

GAO-14-161 Security-Related Assistance to Lebanon

end-use monitoring we observed did not include sufficient information on the physical security of the equipment. Use of the checklists would help ensure that DOD officials document compliance with physical security requirements for defense items transferred to the LAF. Without such documentation, it is not clear whether DOD officials verify physical security safeguards as required by DSCA's manual. In December 2013, DOD officials acknowledged that there had been a gap in the Office of Defense Cooperation's use of the checklists.

State Did Not Consistently Document End-Use Checks for Defense Equipment That Lebanon Purchased Commercially

State's Directorate of Defense Trade Controls administers a program called Blue Lantern to conduct end-use monitoring for defense articles and defense services exported through direct commercial sales. Under the Blue Lantern program, U.S. embassy officials conduct end-use checks by means of a case-by-case review of export license applications against established criteria or "warning flags" for determining potential risks. Embassy officials primarily conduct two types of end-use monitoring checks: prelicense checks prior to issuance of a license and postshipment checks after an export has been approved and shipped.[26]

- Prelicense checks: A prelicense check may be requested to (1) confirm the bona fides of an unfamiliar consignee or end-user; (2) ensure that details of a proposed transaction match those identified on a license application; (3) confirm that the end-user listed on the license application has ordered the items in question; (4) verify the security of facilities where items may be permanently or temporarily housed; and (5) help to ensure that the foreign party understands its responsibilities under U.S. regulations and law.
- Postshipment checks: The Directorate of Defense Trade Controls may request a postshipment check in order to (1) confirm that the party or parties named on the license received the licensed items exported from the United States; (2) determine whether the items have been or are being used in accordance with the provisions of that license; (3) identify any parties involved in the transaction that are not listed on the license application; and (4) determine the specific use and handling of the exported articles, or other issues related to the transaction.

---

[26]State also occasionally conducts checks after a license has been issued but before the items have been shipped if new information comes to light indicating possible concerns about a transaction that were not known at the time the license was approved.

State's Blue Lantern guidebook provides instructions to U.S. diplomatic posts on how to conduct Blue Lantern end-use monitoring, including reporting and documentation requirements.[27] For example, the guide specifies the type of information that should be included in cables from the overseas posts in response to an inquiry from State.

In fiscal years 2007 through 2012, State conducted 15 Blue Lantern end-use monitoring checks for equipment—mostly firearms for the ISF—authorized for export to Lebanon through direct commercial sales.[28] State reported favorable results for 14 of the Blue Lantern checks and unfavorable results for one.[29]

On the basis of our review of State documents and interviews with U.S. officials in Washington, D.C., and Beirut, we determined that State officials in headquarters and at the U.S. Embassy in Beirut did not always document the results of the Blue Lantern checks consistent with guidance specified in State's Blue Lantern guidebook. According to the guidebook, all Blue Lantern requests are sent by cable to the U.S. embassy or consulate in the country or countries involved in the transaction. The guidebook specifies that Blue Lantern cables prepared by the U.S. mission in response to the request should describe specific actions taken and results of the inquiry, including identification of persons interviewed; description of documents or equipment reviewed; difficulties incurred; degree of cooperation by the end-users, consignees, or both; and recommendations for State action, if appropriate. According to the guidebook, the U.S. mission should maintain detailed records regarding the Blue Lantern cases as a resource to facilitate future checks and to brief new staff on how to conduct the checks.

To assess State's compliance with its Blue Lantern guidance, we selected a judgmental sample of all 10 Blue Lantern checks for equipment exported or intended for export to Lebanon in fiscal years 2010 through 2012 and requested copies of the cables associated with those checks.

---

[27] Department of Defense, Directorate of Defense Trade Controls, *Blue Lantern: A Guide to End-Use Monitoring of Defense Articles and Services Exported via Commercial Channels* (Washington, D.C.: July 2010).

[28] Two cases were not completed. No defense articles were involved.

[29] During this same period, State approved a total of about 200 licenses for direct commercial sales of defense articles to Lebanon.

State documented the details of 5 of the 10 checks in diplomatic cables and 1 in e-mail messages. For the 4 remaining Blue Lantern checks, State officials informed us that the requests from headquarters and the responses from the embassy were made by e-mail. We asked for copies of the e-mails, but State officials told us that the e-mails were no longer in State's information system. A State official noted that the Blue Lantern database had case summaries based on the e-mails. However, the summary information in the database consisted of notes that did not always contain all the required information specified in State's guidance. For example, the summary information for the cases in which the e-mails were no longer available showed that the embassy officials met with the ISF but did not identify the officials interviewed. Without the information specified in the guidebook, State may not have information it needs to fully inform future checks and train new staff. State said in February 2014 that the U. S. Embassy in Beirut has established a policy requiring all Blue Lantern responses to be sent via cable to Washington, D.C., in order to ensure that there is a permanent record of the Embassy's response to a Blue Lantern check. However, State did not provide support this statement.

State's INL Inventories Equipment Provided to the ISF but May Not Be Ensuring That Recipients Implement Recommended Physical Security Safeguards for Defense Articles

As required by INL's End-Use Monitoring Program, INL officials conduct an annual inventory by serial number of equipment that INL has provided to the ISF. This equipment typically includes office furniture, vehicles, and computer equipment but may also include boats, training firearms, and police vehicles. (See fig. 5 for photographs of equipment INL provided to the ISF.) INL personnel said they had attached barcodes to the equipment and we observed them use a scanner to inventory the equipment. The 2012 INL inventory report for Lebanon shows that INL personnel inspected about 78 percent of 1,243 items provided to the Lebanese security forces. INL personnel may also inspect items by secondary means including comparing inventory records and consulting with host government officials.

Figure □ P□otogra□□s o□□S□□□ui□□ent Pro□ided to Lebanon□s □nternal Security □orces

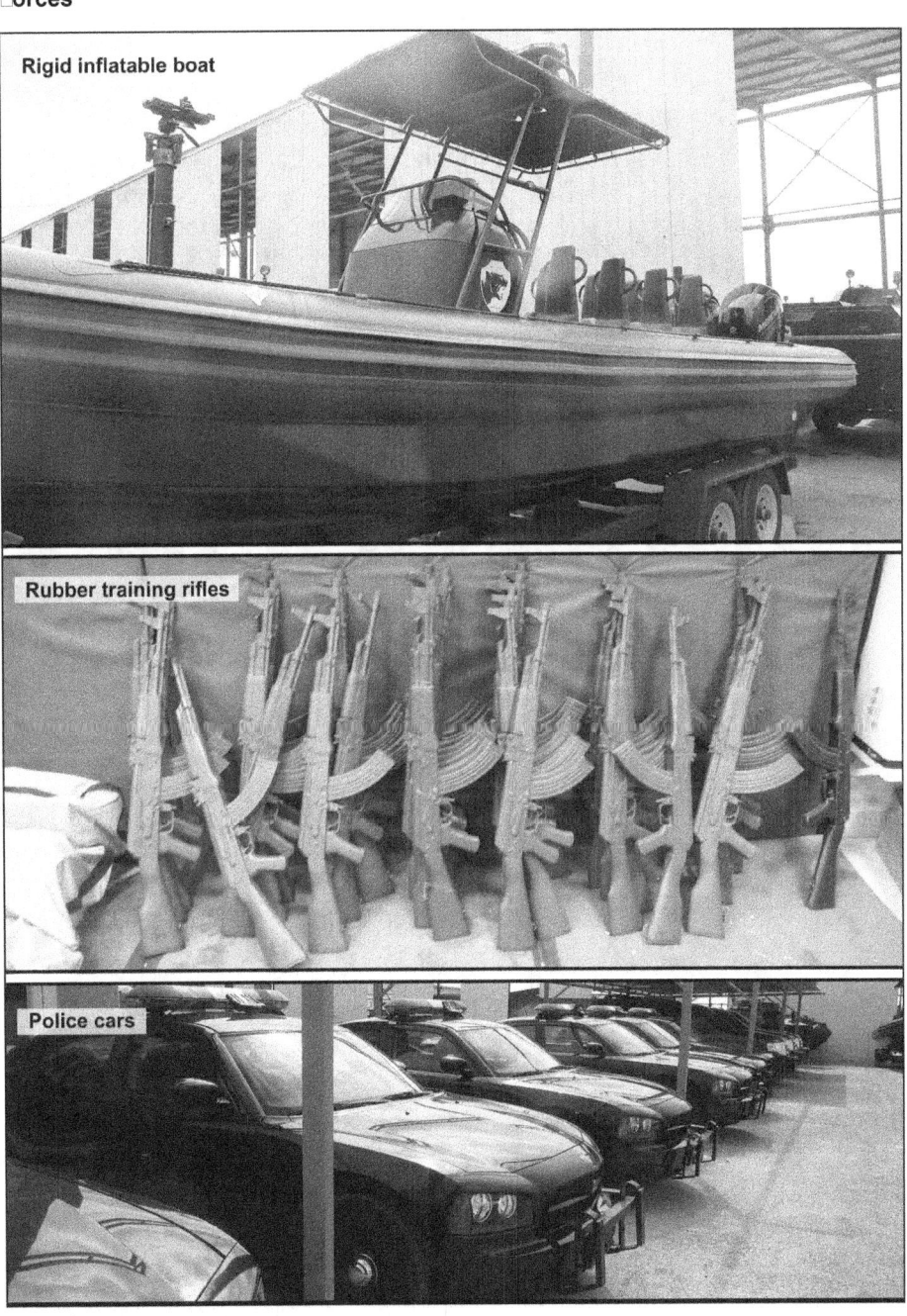

Source: GAO.

While INL officials annually inventory all equipment INL has provided to the ISF, INL may not be ensuring that the ISF is implementing recommended physical security safeguards for defense articles because INL lacks procedures to identify defense articles and the recommended safeguards for storing them. In May 2013, we asked INL officials if any of the equipment INL had provided to Lebanon were defense articles. Though INL officials first told us that they had provided no defense articles or any other controlled items to Lebanon, in August 2013 INL provided us with its formal response confirming that it had provided two defense articles to the ISF—night vision devices and ceramic plates for bullet proof vests. With regard to these two articles, we found the following:

- INL consulted with the directorate only one of the two times it sought to transfer defense articles to Lebanon during the period covered by our review. While INL did not have formal procedures for identifying defense articles, INL officials stated that their practice is to contact State's Directorate of Defense Trade Controls, which licenses direct commercial sales of defense articles, when providing equipment pursuant to a certain license exception. In 2012, INL consulted with the directorate to confirm that no export license would be required for the provision of night vision devices to the Government of Lebanon.[30] In the directorate's memo back to INL confirming that no license was required, INL was informed of physical security safeguards that the directorate recommended that the INL should direct the ISF to implement as conditions for a transfer of night vision devices to the ISF. However, INL did not consult the directorate about ceramic plates, which INL provided for bullet proof vests that it transferred to the ISF in February 2013 under the license exception. This was the only other case that INL identified in which it provided a defense article to the ISF. Although INL did not consult with the directorate about the ceramic plates, INL officials said that INL would contact the directorate in the future about any defense articles it planned to transfer to the ISF.

---

[30]According to a July 2012 memorandum prepared in response, the Directorate of Defense Trade Controls indicated that INL could transfer the equipment without a license under Section 38 (b)(2) of the Arms Export Control Act, which states that no export license shall be required for exports by or for any agency of the U.S. government for carrying out a foreign assistance or sales program authorized by law and subject to control by the President by other means. The "control by the President by other means" in this case was the ability to monitor and control procurements to the ISF through end-use monitoring by the U.S. Embassy in Beirut.

- INL lacked written procedures to determine what physical security safeguards are recommended for defense articles. INL officials said that the ISF secures INL-provided equipment and guards the facilities where it is stored. According to embassy officials in Beirut, there are no INL requirements for inspecting the ISF facilities where U.S.-provided equipment is stored. However, when INL consulted the Directorate of Defense Trade Controls about the transfer of night vision devices to the ISF, the directorate recommended that INL place 10 conditions on the transfer. These conditions included 5 technical parameters setting limitations on the performance of key components of the night vision devices, such as the brightness and resolution of their image intensifier tubes, and 5 physical security safeguards that the ISF should implement, such as storing the devices in a secured, locked facility. State officials in Washington, D.C., said that, although the conditions communicated by the directorate to the INL were not requirements, embassy officials would, in the future, inspect ISF facilities to see that the recommended physical security safeguards were being implemented. Nonetheless, in the absence of written procedures, it is unclear what procedures INL would follow for future transfers of defense articles. Moreover, INL communicated the conditions of the transfer of night vision devices to the ISF only in September 2013, after transferring the equipment in August 2013. Communicating conditions for physical security safeguards to the ISF after delivery of the equipment could lessen INL's ability to determine whether the ISF implements those safeguards.

In response to our inquiries on its plans to address potential gaps in physical security safeguards for defense articles, INL stated in January 2014 that it would update its Acquisition Handbook to document new policies. State anticipates that changes to the handbook would require INL to inform the Directorate of Defense Trade Controls of INL's decision to procure and provide equipment without an export license, as allowed under Section 38(b)(2) of the Arms Export Control Act. However, it is unclear whether these revisions would establish procedures to (1) identify when items are defense articles and (2) determine if physical security safeguards are recommended.

U.S. Government Has Vetted Lebanese Recipients for Human Rights Violations Prior to Providing Assistance

State's 2012 Guide to Vetting Policy and Process—a primary source of guidance for U.S. personnel responsible for implementing the Leahy laws—requires State officials in Washington, D.C., and overseas to vet for potential human rights violations all individuals or units nominated to receive training or equipment by checking their names against files, databases, and other sources of information.[31] In detailing the steps for vetting, the guidance specifies that relevant data are to be entered into the International Vetting and Security Tracking (INVEST) database.[32] INVEST is State's official system of record for conducting Leahy vetting and recording compliance with the Leahy laws. State requires human rights vetting through INVEST unless the individual or unit has already been vetted within the prior year, according to a State official. State approves, suspends, or denies the requests for training as a result of its vetting efforts.[33] Our review of State's INVEST database showed that State vetted almost 10,000 individuals and units in Lebanon that applied for U.S. training from October 10, 2010, through April 30, 2013. The majority (77 percent), applied for INCLE training (see figure 6). By cross-checking a random sample of names from six rosters for U.S. training delivered to Lebanese security force individuals or units against State's designated vetting database, we found that all the names in the sample had been vetted for human rights violations before the individuals received the training, as required.

---

[31] See Department of State, *Compliance with the State and DOD Leahy Laws: A Guide to Vetting Policy and Process* (Washington, D.C.: September 2012).

[32] INVEST was launched in Lebanon on October 10, 2010. Prior to the implementation of INVEST, State used cables to communicate vetting requests and results between State headquarters in Washington, D.C., and U.S. embassies around the world.

[33] To suspend is to withdraw a candidate from consideration. In some instances, the post withdraws a name due to non-Leahy-specific grounds, such as suspicion of involvement in narcotics or corruption.

Figure 6 Percentage of Lebanese Candidates That Applied for U.S Security-Related Training by Funding Source

5%
7%
12%
77%   International Narcotics Control and Law Enforcement

International Military Education and Training
Other types of training
Antiterrorism Assistance

Source: GAO analysis of State data.

Notes: Percentages do not sum to 100 because of rounding. Included in data were all individuals and units in Lebanon that applied for U.S. security-related training from October 10, 2010, through April 30, 2013—a total of almost 10,000 candidates.

State approved training for approximately 93 percent of the candidates and disallowed training for the remaining 7 percent for whom the vetting process produced a suspension. While administrative reasons accounted for most of the suspensions, such as a name submitted with insufficient time for vetting clearance prior to the class start date, potential human rights violations accounted for a few suspensions.[34] U.S. officials in Beirut communicated suspensions based on human rights violations to Lebanese government officials. Administrative reasons for some suspensions were not communicated to the Lebanese government because the U.S. officials did not think they were required to do so. In

---

[34]Other administrative reasons recorded for suspensions in Lebanon included the following: vetting was not required, incorrect names, or the course was cancelled, according to INVEST case notes as of May 21, 2013.

GAO-14-161 Security-Related Assistance to Lebanon

September 2013, we reported that State guidance to embassies on the human rights vetting process did not specify whether the requirement to inform foreign governments applies when a unit or individual is suspended from receiving assistance.[35] Hence, we recommended that State provide clarifying guidance for implementing the duty-to-inform requirement of the State Leahy law, such as guidance on whether U.S. embassies should or should not notify a foreign government in cases of suspensions.[36] On the basis of evidence presented in a June 2013 Human Rights Watch report on Lebanon, in August 2013, State issued its first denial for training to individuals from the Drugs Repression Bureau of the ISF and informed ISF about this denial.[37] As a result of the denial, three Lebanese counternarcotics officials were not approved for a September 2013 training course. Officials of the U.S. Embassy in Beirut communicated the reasons for the denial to the ISF during the course of our review.[38]

On the basis of our cross-check analysis of a sample of names from six training rosters against INVEST data, we estimated that State vetted for potential human rights violations all Lebanese students who attended security forces training from October 10, 2010, through April 30, 2013. We selected a random sample of 118 names from training rosters from the Lebanese Armed Forces; INCLE; Antiterrorism Assistance and other Nonproliferation, Antiterrorism, Demining, and Related programs; and International Military Education and Training. We cross-checked those names with the names of all Lebanese candidates vetted for human rights violations through INVEST from October 10, 2010, through April 30, 2013. Results of our analysis show that all 118 names on the training rosters were also found in INVEST. Therefore, we estimate that 100 percent of the 7,104 Lebanese students that attended U.S. training during that

---

[35]State's guidance notes that a unit or individual should be suspended if the embassy cannot confirm or rule out the derogatory information found on a unit or individual in time to accommodate a training event.

[36]See GAO-13-866.

[37]Human Rights Watch, *"It's Part of the Job": Ill-treatment and Torture of Vulnerable Groups in Lebanese Police Stations* (June 2013).

[38]In response to an official letter from U.S. Embassy in Beirut, the ISF launched a number of conferences and training courses on human rights and opened an investigation into the content of the Human Rights Watch report.

period were vetted for human rights violations through INVEST before they received training (see table 3).[39]

Table 3: Population of Lebanese Student Names on Training Rosters and Final Sample of Names Selected for Cross-Checking with International Vetting and Security Tracking Database Records

	Training rosters	Population	Final Sample
1	Foreign Military Financing	423	10
2	International Narcotics Control and Law Enforcement (I)	3,093	39
3	International Narcotics Control and Law Enforcement (II)	3,133	39
4	Antiterrorism Assistance (Nonproliferation, Antiterrorism, Demining, and Related programs)	247	10
5	Other Nonproliferation, Antiterrorism, Demining, and Related programs	10	10
6	International Military Education and Training	198	10
	Total	7,104	118[a]

Source: GAO analysis of State data.

[a]We deleted two names from our original sample of 120 names because the individuals were scheduled to attend a course that occurred prior to October 10, 2010, the date that INVEST was launched in Lebanon.

The U.S. Embassy in Beirut also conducts human rights vetting for units that are to receive equipment. In November 2011, State agreed with our recommendation that it implement individual- and unit-level human rights vetting for all recipients of equipment.[40] As of July 2013, Bureau of Democracy, Human Rights, and Labor officials said that vetting of units that receive equipment is increasing worldwide and that the bureau hopes to achieve State-wide concurrence implementing the recommendation.

State guidance also requires embassies to develop standard operating procedures for human rights vetting. The U.S. Embassy in Beirut developed standard operating procedures to implement State guidance during the course of our review. In September 2013, we found that State does not monitor whether all U.S. embassies have developed standard operating procedures that address the Leahy laws' requirements. Therefore, we recommended, and State agreed, to ensure that all U.S.

[39]We are 95 percent confident that the actual proportion of INVEST names that were properly vetted was at least 97 percent.

[40]See GAO, *Persian Gulf: Implementation Gaps Limit the Effectiveness of End-Use Monitoring and Human Rights Vetting for U.S. Military Equipment*, GAO-12-89 (Washington, D.C.: Nov. 17, 2011).

embassies have standard operating procedures that address human rights vetting requirements in the Leahy laws.[41]

Conclusions

U.S. agencies have allocated hundreds of millions of dollars for equipment and training to the government of Lebanon as part of U.S. efforts to build partner capacity and address threats to U.S. interests. Such efforts remain a U.S. priority. Just as important to the interests of the United States and its partners are efforts to ensure that any provided security-related equipment or training assistance does not help those who wish to do harm to the United States or its partners. Hence, end-use monitoring and human rights vetting are two critical activities that the U.S. government employs in Lebanon and worldwide to prevent misuse of its security-related equipment and training assistance. However, existing implementation gaps may weaken efforts to safeguard some equipment from misuse. These gaps involve embassy officials not utilizing required checklists to verify Lebanese facilities' safeguards for sensitive defense equipment and not documenting details of State's end-use checks. Closing these gaps could help mitigate the impact of security-related travel restrictions on U.S. officials' access to some locations and could also help raise the level of confidence that Lebanese security forces are complying with security requirements. Because end-use monitoring in Lebanon is intended to provide U.S. officials with visibility over the implementation of required safeguards, the above-mentioned gaps reduce the U.S. government's confidence that safeguards are being properly implemented to prevent equipment from falling into the wrong hands. Furthermore, the absence of INL procedures for identifying defense articles erodes confidence that State officials are applying recommended end-use monitoring and security safeguards on defense equipment. On a more positive note, our analysis did confirm that 100 percent of the Lebanese recipients of U.S. training were vetted for human rights violations and that this system appears to be working as intended in Lebanon.

Recommendations for Executive Action

To help ensure that U.S. agencies are in a better position to ensure adequate safeguards for and monitoring of sensitive equipment, we recommend that the Secretary of Defense take additional steps to ensure

---

[41]See GAO-13-866.

that Office of Defense Cooperation officials in Beirut use the checklists required during the physical security checks.

In addition, we recommend that the Secretary of State take the following three actions:

- Direct the Directorate of Defense Trade Controls and U.S. officials overseas to maintain cables or e-mails as required by State guidance to document each Blue Lantern end-use check.
- Direct State bureaus transferring equipment to foreign security forces under security-related assistance programs to establish formal written procedures to identify whether items are defense articles.
- Direct State bureaus transferring equipment to foreign security forces under security-related assistance programs to establish formal written procedures to consult with the Directorate of Defense Trade Controls to determine if there are additional safeguards recommended for the transfer of the defense articles.

Agency Comments and Our Evaluation

We provided a draft of this report to DOD and State for comment. DOD and State provided written comments which are reprinted in appendixes IV and V, respectively. State also provided technical comments, which we have incorporated into the report, as appropriate. In their comments, DOD and State generally concurred with the report's findings and recommendations.

In its written comments, DOD noted that the Office of Defense Cooperation in Beirut has started taking steps to address the recommendation.

In its written comments, State noted that while it agreed with our recommendation that it maintain records of cables and e-mails that document each Blue Lantern end-use check, it disagreed with our finding that it did not adequately do so with regard to Lebanon. State noted that it did document key findings of the four inquiries in the Blue Lantern database, as these cases were adjudicated together as a group involving the same foreign consignee and Lebanese Security Forces. However, as we pointed out in the draft report, the summary information in State's database consisted of notes that did not always contain all the required information specified in State's guidance. For example, the summary information on the four cases showed that the embassy officials met with the ISF but did not identify the officials interviewed. State also noted that the draft referred to defense articles that were "exported" to Lebanon rather than "authorized" for export. We have revised the report accordingly.

As agreed with your office, unless you publicly announce the contents of this report earlier, we plan no further distribution until five days from the report date. At that time, we will send copies of this report to appropriate congressional committees; the Secretary of Defense; the Secretary of State; and other interested parties. In addition, the report will be available at no charge on the GAO website at http://www.gao.gov.

If you or your staff have any questions about this report, please contact me at (202) 512-7331 or johnsoncm@gao.gov. Contact points for our Offices of Congressional Relations and Public Affairs may be found on the last page of this report. GAO staff who made key contributions to this report are listed in appendix VI.

Sincerely yours,

Charles Michael Johnson, Jr.
Director, International Affairs and Trade

Appendix I: Scope and Methodology

The objectives of this review were to assess the extent to which the U.S. government (1) disbursed or committed funds allocated for Lebanese security forces in fiscal years 2009 through 2013, (2) implemented end-use monitoring for equipment transferred to Lebanese security forces, and (3) vetted Lebanese recipients of U.S. security-related training for human rights violations. To address these objectives, we obtained funding data from the Department of Defense (DOD) and the Department of State (State) on programs that provide security-related assistance to Lebanon. We also analyzed documents from DOD and State, such as cables, manuals, handbooks, compliance and inventory reports, and data on U.S.-provided equipment, training, and end-use checks, among others. We interviewed U.S. officials in Washington, D.C.; at the U.S. Central Command in Tampa, Florida; and at the U.S. Embassy in Beirut, Lebanon, as well as officials of the Lebanese Armed Forces (LAF) and Internal Security Forces (ISF) in Beirut, Lebanon.

To assess the extent to which the U.S. government has disbursed or committed security-related assistance funding for Lebanon's security forces since fiscal year 2009, we requested data from State and DOD. The funding data we report represent the balances as of September 30, 2013. State provided data on the status of allocations, obligations, unobligated balances, and disbursements for all of the funding accounts that support security-related assistance in Lebanon: Foreign Military Financing; International Narcotics Control and Law Enforcement; International Military Education and Training; and Nonproliferation, Antiterrorism, Demining and Related Programs; and Section 1206 and 1207 authorities. State collected the data directly from each bureau for State-implemented accounts and from DOD for Foreign Military Financing and International Military Education and Training. However, because Foreign Military Financing funds are budgeted and tracked in a different way than other foreign assistance accounts, DOD provided us with data on commitments. Recognizing that different agencies and bureaus may use slightly different accounting terms, we provided each agency with the definitions from GAO's A Glossary of Terms Used in the Federal Budget Process[1] and requested that each agency provide the relevant data according to those definitions. We also discussed the types of assistance provided with various officials of the LAF and the ISF. To assess the

---

[1]GAO, *A Glossary of Terms Used in the Federal Budget Process*, GAO-05-734SP (Washington, D.C.: September 2005).

reliability of the data provided, we requested and reviewed information from officials from each agency regarding the agency's underlying financial data system(s) and the checks, controls, and reviews used to ensure the accuracy and reliability of the data provided. We determined that the data provided were sufficiently reliable for the purposes of this report.

To assess the extent to which the U.S. government has implemented end-use monitoring for equipment provided to Lebanese security forces, we reviewed relevant laws and regulations, DOD and State policy guidance, and reports and other documents; analyzed equipment and end-use monitoring data and reports; and interviewed officials from DOD, State, the LAF, and the ISF.

For DOD's Golden Sentry program, we reviewed policy and guidance documents, including the Defense Security Cooperation Agency's Security Assistance Management Manual, the Office of Defense Cooperation-Beirut's Standard Operating Procedures, the Security Cooperation Information Portal End-Use Monitoring Customer Assistance Handbook, and U.S. Central Command regulations. We also obtained and analyzed the 2012 Compliance Assessment Visit to Lebanon report, U.S. Central Command Inspector General Report for the Office of Defense Cooperation-Beirut, annual end-use monitoring reports for Lebanon, reports of lost or destroyed U.S. equipment provided to Lebanon, Lebanese compliance plans for safeguarding U.S. equipment, and security checklists required for enhanced end-use equipment in Lebanon. In addition, we reviewed and analyzed data and management reports on the equipment provided to Lebanon and end-use checks. Specifically, we reviewed management reports from DOD's Security Cooperation Information Portal database, including delinquent, reconciliation, ad-hoc, and trend reports. We used the portal database to identify defense articles provided to Lebanon that require routine and enhanced end-use monitoring and the compliance actions taken for the items. We compared the data on defense articles and end-use monitoring to the various management reports and found the data to be sufficiently reliable for our purposes. Using the data provided by DOD, we drew a nongeneralizable random sample of 30 items for physical inspection out of 184 items that required enhanced end-use monitoring at two locations in Beirut, Lebanon. During our fieldwork at one of the locations, we observed DOD officials conducting enhanced end-use monitoring checks. In addition, we interviewed DOD officials with the Defense Security Cooperation Agency, U.S. Central Command, U.S. Special Operations

Command, and the U.S. Embassy in Beirut. In Lebanon, we also met with officials from the LAF and the ISF.

For State's Blue Lantern program, we reviewed the Blue Lantern guidebook.[2] We reviewed and analyzed Direct Commercial Sales license data, and Blue Lantern checks for Lebanon from fiscal years 2007 through 2012. Although State conducted 15 checks between fiscal years 2007 and 2012, we analyzed only the 10 Blue Lantern checks conducted in fiscal years 2011 and 2012. We limited our analysis to checks during these years to increase the likelihood that the embassy officials who conducted these checks would still be in their current positions, thereby enabling further discussion about the specific details of the checks. We requested both outgoing and responding cables for each of the 10 checks; State was unable to provide cables or email communication for 4 of the 10 Blue Lantern checks. Based on summary information provided for each check and cables and e-mail correspondence on 7 of the 10 checks, we analyzed and recorded information about each case, including the subject of the check, the commodity checked, license conditions, evidence that site visits were or were not requested and conducted, inventories requested and conducted, and any follow-up that post indicated was necessary. We determined the Blue Lantern data to be sufficiently reliable for our purposes. In addition, we interviewed State officials in the Bureau of Political and Military Affairs, the Bureau of Near Eastern Affairs, the Office of Foreign Assistance, and the Directorate of Defense Trade Controls in Washington, D.C., as well as officials at the U.S. Embassy in Beirut.

For State's Bureau of International Narcotics and Law Enforcement Affairs (INL), we reviewed policy and procedure guidelines for end-use monitoring. We obtained and analyzed inventory lists of equipment that INL provided to Lebanon's security forces during fiscal years 2007 through 2012, data extracted from the Integrated Logistics Management System database. We received a demonstration on the use of this database to record annual inspection and inventory of equipment. In addition, we reviewed annual inspection reports submitted by embassy officials, Letters of Offer and Acceptance, and a sample transfer letter that contained inspection requirements. In addition, we toured two ISF

[2]Department of State, Directorate of Defense Trade Controls, *Blue Lantern: A Guide to End-Use Monitoring of Defense Articles and Services Exported via Commercial Channels* (Washington, D.C.: July 2010).

facilities in Beirut, Lebanon, and observed INL-provided equipment. Lastly, we interviewed State officials of the Bureaus Political and Military Affairs, International Narcotics and Law Enforcement Affairs, and Near Eastern Affairs; the Office of Foreign Assistance; the Directorate of Defense Trade Controls; and the U.S. Embassy in Beirut.

To assess the extent to which the U.S. government vetted Lebanese recipients of U.S. security-related training for potential human rights violations, we interviewed DOD and State officials, reviewed both agencies' vetting guidance, and analyzed State documents from Lebanon on individuals and units vetted. We interviewed officials from State's Bureau of Democracy, Human Rights, and Labor and Bureau of Near Eastern Affairs who are responsible for overseeing the human rights vetting process and answering questions from vetting personnel at the U.S. Embassy in Beirut. In Lebanon, we also met with U.S. embassy officials from DOD and State, and also relevant officials from the Department of Justice and the U.S. Agency for International Development to understand these other agencies' roles in the human rights vetting process. We also met with representatives of the LAF and ISF to understand their familiarity with the Leahy laws and the U.S. human rights vetting process, as well as how the U.S. Embassy in Beirut communicates vetting results to them. In addition, we reviewed State's human rights vetting guidance, including the Leahy human rights vetting guide; the International Vetting and Security Tracking (INVEST) user guide; multiple cables from State communicating directives to embassies regarding the implementation of the State and DOD Leahy laws; and a Joint Staff message issued by DOD in June 2004 that provided guidance on human rights verification for DOD-funded training of foreign security forces.

Furthermore, we reviewed the State and DOD Leahy laws, as well as the U.S. Embassy in Beirut's standard operating procedures. Lastly, to assess whether or not Lebanese students who attended training were previously vetted for potential human rights violations, we analyzed data from State's INVEST database on almost 10,000 Lebanese individuals or units vetted from October 10, 2010, through April 30, 2013. We requested, obtained, and reviewed six training rosters with about 7,100 names of Lebanese students that attended training from October 1, 2010, to April 30, 2013, provided by these security-related assistance programs: International Military Education and Training; International Narcotics Control and Law Enforcement; and Nonproliferation, Antiterrorism, Demining, and Related programs. We selected a random sample of 118 Lebanese names that included representation from all rosters, with a minimum of 10 sampled names per roster. We provided this list of names to the Bureau of Democracy, Human Rights, and Labor and observed as a bureau official entered the first and last name into the search feature of INVEST. If the name was found, we then confirmed other fields, such as the date and description of the training, or the rank of the trainee. Despite some spelling variations, all 118 names of students were found in INVEST. Therefore, we estimate that 100 percent of the Lebanese recipients of training were vetted. The 95 percent margin of error on this estimate is 3 percentage points.

We conducted this performance audit from April 2013 to February 2014 in accordance with generally accepted government auditing standards. Those standards require that we plan and perform the audit to obtain sufficient, appropriate evidence to provide a reasonable basis for our findings and conclusions based on our audit objectives. We believe that the evidence obtained provides a reasonable basis for our findings and conclusions based on our audit objectives.

Appendix II: U.S. Human Rights Vetting Process

To address both the State and DOD Leahy laws and determine whether there is credible information of a gross violation of human rights, State has established a U.S. human rights vetting process. The State-led process, as illustrated in figure 7, consists of vetting by personnel representing selected agencies and State offices at (1) the U.S. Embassy in Beirut and State headquarters in Washington, D.C.; (2) State's Bureau of Democracy, Human Rights, and Labor; and (3) State's Bureau of Near Eastern Affairs. The personnel involved in the vetting process screen prospective recipients of assistance by searching relevant files, databases, and other sources of information for credible information about gross violations of human rights. State processes, documents, and tracks human rights vetting requests and results through its International Vetting and Security Tracking system (INVEST), a web-based database.[1] The Bureau of Democracy, Human Rights, and Labor is responsible for overseeing the vetting process and for developing human rights vetting polices, among other duties.

---

[1]State began implementing INVEST in Beirut on October 10, 2010. Before implementing INVEST, State used cables to communicate vetting requests and results between State headquarters in Washington, D.C., and the U.S. Embassy in Beirut.

GAO-14-161 Security-Related Assistance to Lebanon

Figure 7: Security Rights Vetting Process

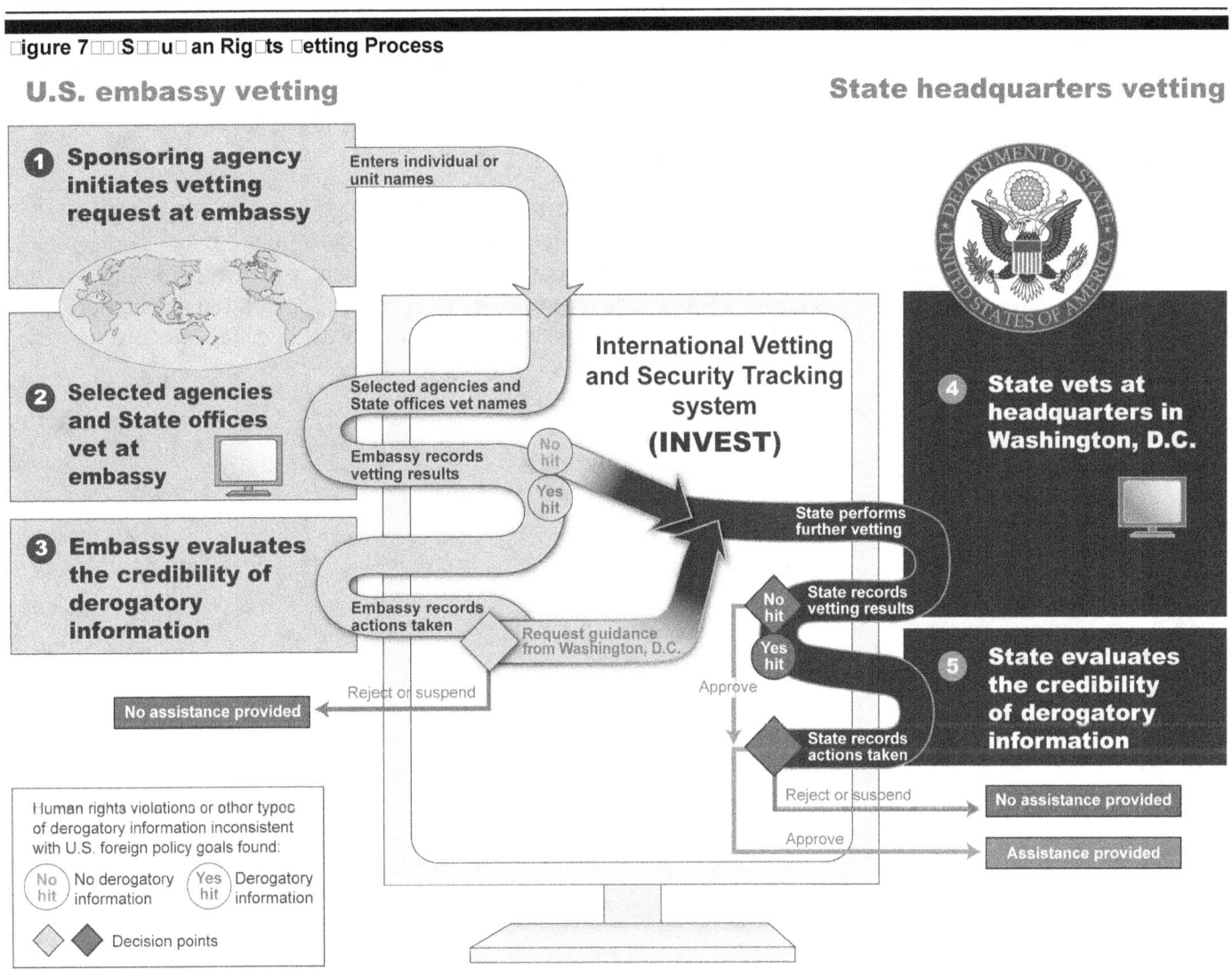

Sources: GAO analysis of State documentation; Map Resources (map).

Appendix III: Status of Funds for U.S. Security-Related Assistance Programs for Lebanon

The Department of Defense (DOD) and Department of State (State) allocated $671 million in security-related assistance for Lebanon in fiscal years 2009 through 2013, with funds varying by year and program. The agencies utilized eight programs to provide this security-related assistance: Foreign Military Financing, International Narcotics Control and Law Enforcement, Section 1206, International Military Education and Training, Antiterrorism Assistance, Counterterrorism Financing, Export Control and Related Border Security, and Section 1207. See figures 8 through 15 for details on allocation, obligation, and disbursement, or commitment of funds for each program's security-related assistance provided to Lebanon in fiscal years 2009 through 2013. Data are as of September 30, 2013.

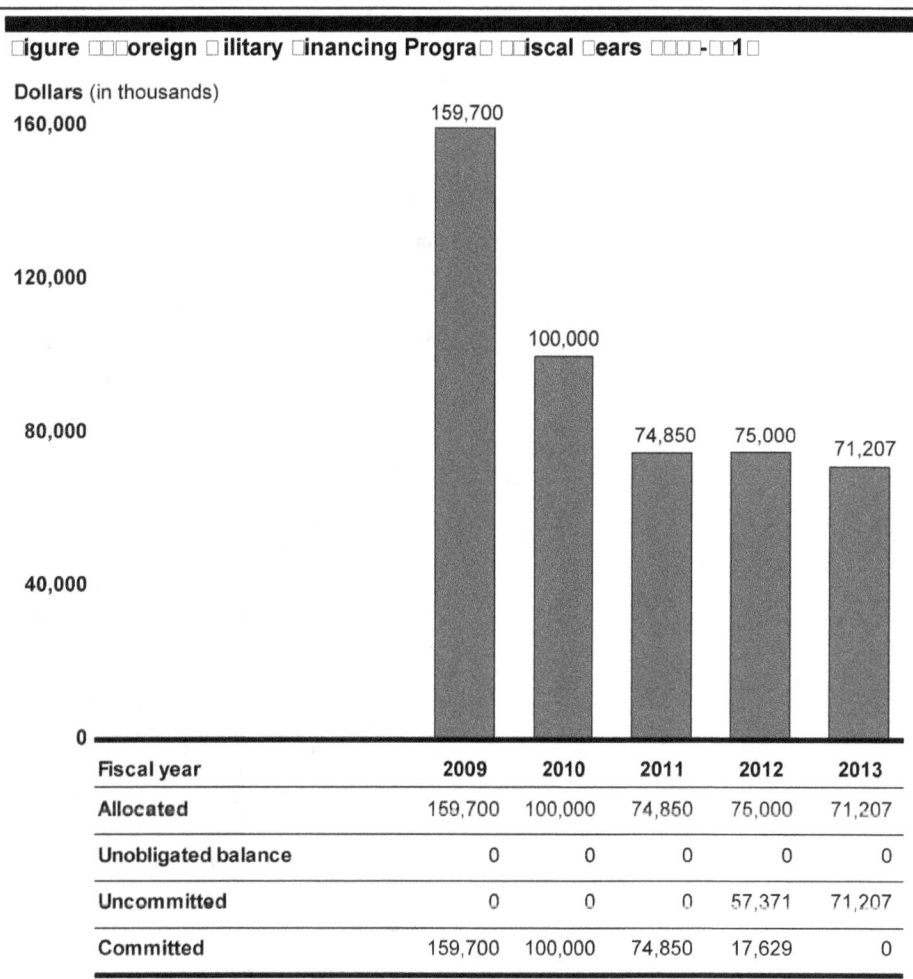

Figure 8: Foreign Military Financing Program, Fiscal Years 2009-2013

Dollars (in thousands)

Fiscal year	2009	2010	2011	2012	2013
Allocated	159,700	100,000	74,850	75,000	71,207
Unobligated balance	0	0	0	0	0
Uncommitted	0	0	0	57,371	71,207
Committed	159,700	100,000	74,850	17,629	0

Source: GAO analysis of State and DOD data.

Notes: We were not able to present data on Foreign Military Financing (FMF) for Lebanon in the same way as for the other programs because FMF funds are budgeted and tracked differently and the system used does not track FMF information consistent with the way we are presenting the data for the other programs. For the purposes of this report, "uncommitted" amounts represent FMF obligations not yet committed for expenditure and "committed" amounts include FMF funding that has been committed but not yet disbursed, as well as FMF funding that has been disbursed to a case. This funding is available for obligation for 1 year, and annual appropriations for FMF generally have contained language stating that FMF funds shall be obligated upon apportionment. For the most recent appropriations containing this language, see the Consolidated Appropriations Act, 2014, Pub. L. No. 113-76, January 17, 2014. Once the period of availability for new obligations expires, the funds are available for an additional 5 years to liquidate obligations.

Figure 9: International Narcotics Control and Law Enforcement Program, Fiscal Years 2009-2013

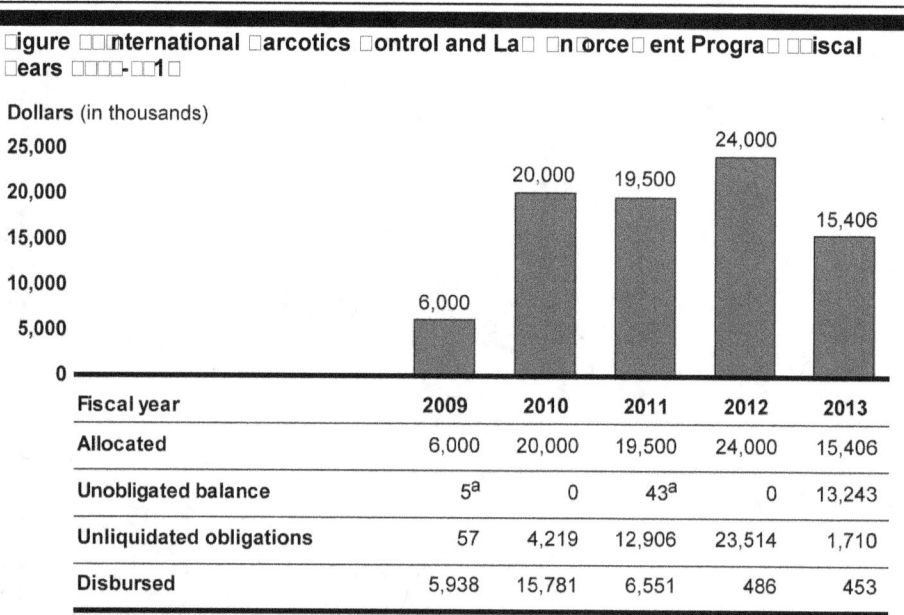

Dollars (in thousands)

Fiscal year	2009	2010	2011	2012	2013
Allocated	6,000	20,000	19,500	24,000	15,406
Unobligated balance	5[a]	0	43[a]	0	13,243
Unliquidated obligations	57	4,219	12,906	23,514	1,710
Disbursed	5,938	15,781	6,551	486	453

Source: GAO analysis of State data.

Notes: International Narcotics Control and Law Enforcement (INCLE) funds are generally available for obligation for 2 years. Once the period of availability for new obligations expires, the funds are available for an additional 5 years to liquidate the obligations. The period of availability for obligations of INCLE funds may be extended for an additional 4 years in certain cases. Pursuant to authority generally provided in the annual Department of State, Foreign Operations, and Related Programs Appropriations Act, certain funds that have been deobligated remain available for obligation for an additional 4 years from the date on which the availability of such funds would otherwise expire if the funds were initially obligated before they would have expired.

[a]According to State, unobligated balances in fiscal years 2009 and 2011 are no longer available for obligation.

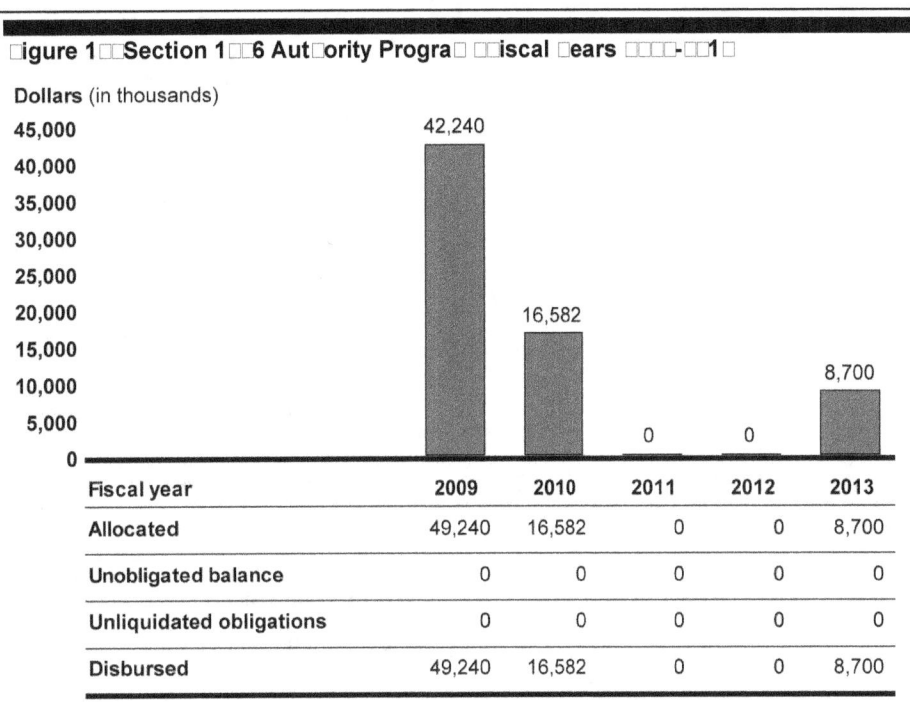

Figure 1: Section 1206 Authority Program Fiscal Years 2009-2013

Dollars (in thousands)

Fiscal year	2009	2010	2011	2012	2013
Allocated	49,240	16,582	0	0	8,700
Unobligated balance	0	0	0	0	0
Unliquidated obligations	0	0	0	0	0
Disbursed	49,240	16,582	0	0	8,700

Source: GAO analysis of State and DOD data.

Notes: State and DOD jointly administer Section 1206 assistance. Funded from the DOD operations and maintenance accounts, Section 1206 funds remain available for 1 year for obligation. Once the period of availability for new obligations expires, the funds are available for an additional 5 years to liquidate the obligations.

⬚igure 11⬚⬚nternational ⬚ilitary ⬚ducation and ⬚raining Progra⬚ ⬚iscal ⬚ears ⬚⬚⬚-⬚⬚1⬚

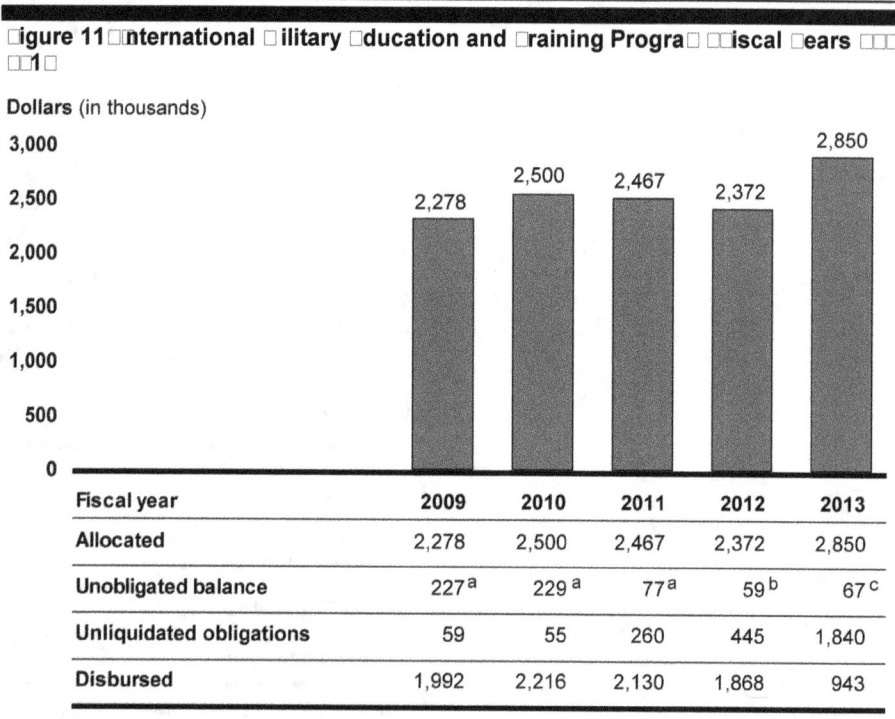

Dollars (in thousands)

Fiscal year	2009	2010	2011	2012	2013
Allocated	2,278	2,500	2,467	2,372	2,850
Unobligated balance	227[a]	229[a]	77[a]	59[b]	67[c]
Unliquidated obligations	59	55	260	445	1,840
Disbursed	1,992	2,216	2,130	1,868	943

Source: GAO analysis of State data.

Notes: The Department of State's (State) Bureau for Political-Military Affairs manages the International Military Education and Training (IMET) budget with input from the Department of Defense's Defense Security Cooperation Agency, which implements the program. According to State officials, the differences between the data we are reporting here for IMET and the data we reported in GAO-13-289 are due to a different methodology that State used for identifying the data. See GAO, *Security Assistance: Evaluations Needed to Determine Effectiveness of U.S. Aid to Lebanon's Security Forces*, GAO-13-289 (Washington, D.C.: Mar.19, 2013).

[a]According to State officials, the unobligated balances for fiscal years 2009, 2010, and 2011 are still available for obligation because these funds are available until expended pursuant to congressionally provided authority that allows up to $4 million annually from IMET funding to remain available until expended subject to regular notification procedures of the Committees on Appropriations.

[b]According to State officials, the unobligated balances for fiscal year 2012 are no longer available for obligation.

[c]The unobligated balance for fiscal year 2013 is still available for obligation until the end of 2014 because, according to State, these funds are part of a portion of the congressional appropriation for IMET that Congress authorized to remain available for 2 years.

⬜igure 1⬜⬜⬜A⬜R⬜Antiterroris⬜ Assistance Progra⬜ ⬜⬜iscal ⬜ears ⬜⬜⬜-⬜⬜1⬜

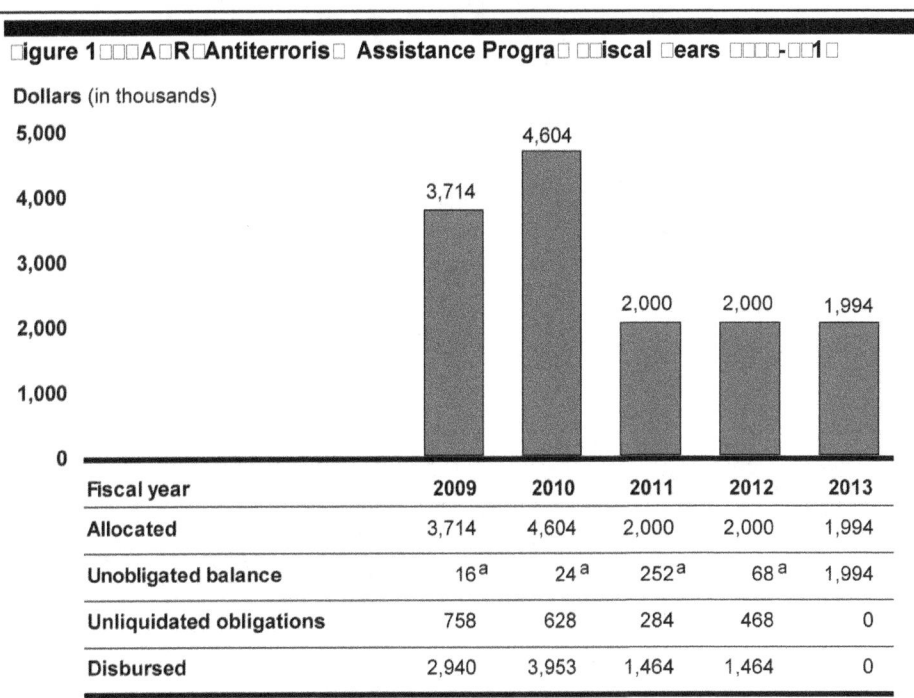

Fiscal year	2009	2010	2011	2012	2013
Allocated	3,714	4,604	2,000	2,000	1,994
Unobligated balance	16[a]	24[a]	252[a]	68[a]	1,994
Unliquidated obligations	758	628	284	468	0
Disbursed	2,940	3,953	1,464	1,464	0

NADR = Nonproliferation, Antiterrorism, Demining, and Related Programs

Source: GAO analysis of State data.

Notes:

NADR funding supports the Antiterrorism Assistance program, which is managed and implemented by State with some implementation by a broader set of agencies.

NADR Antiterrorism Assistance funds are generally available for obligation for 2 years. The availability of NADR funds may be extended for an additional 4 years in some cases. Pursuant to authority generally provided in the annual Department of State, Foreign Operations, and Related Programs Appropriations Act, certain funds that have been deobligated remain available for obligation for an additional 4 years from the date on which the availability of such funds would otherwise expire if the funds were initially obligated before they would have expired. All NADR obligations continue to be available for expenditure for an additional 5 years after the end of their period of availability for obligation.

[a]According to State, unobligated balances in fiscal years 2009, 2010, 2011, and 2012 are no longer available for obligation.

Figure 1: NADR Counterterrorism Financing Program, Fiscal Years 2009-2013

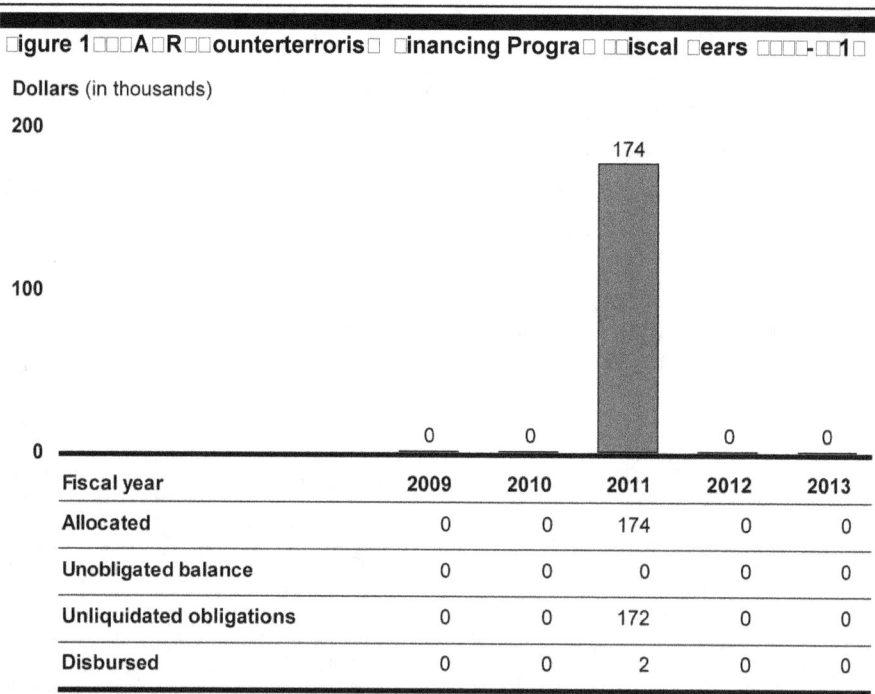

Dollars (in thousands)

Fiscal year	2009	2010	2011	2012	2013
Allocated	0	0	174	0	0
Unobligated balance	0	0	0	0	0
Unliquidated obligations	0	0	172	0	0
Disbursed	0	0	2	0	0

NADR = Nonproliferation, Antiterrorism, Demining, and Related Programs

Source: GAO analysis of State data.

Notes:

NADR funding supports the Counterterrorism Financing program, which is managed and implemented by State with some implementation by a broader set of agencies.

NADR Counterterrorism Financing funds are generally available for obligation for 2 years. All NADR obligations continue to be available for expenditure for an additional 5 years after the end of their period of availability for obligation.

In our prior report, State reported that it had allocated $166,000 for the Counterterrorism Financing program in fiscal year 2011. See GAO-13-289. The $174,000 State is currently reporting for fiscal year 2011 includes Lebanon-specific costs incurred as part of a regional training program that was not included in the first report.

Figure 14: NADR Export Control and Related Border Security Program Fiscal Years 2009-2013

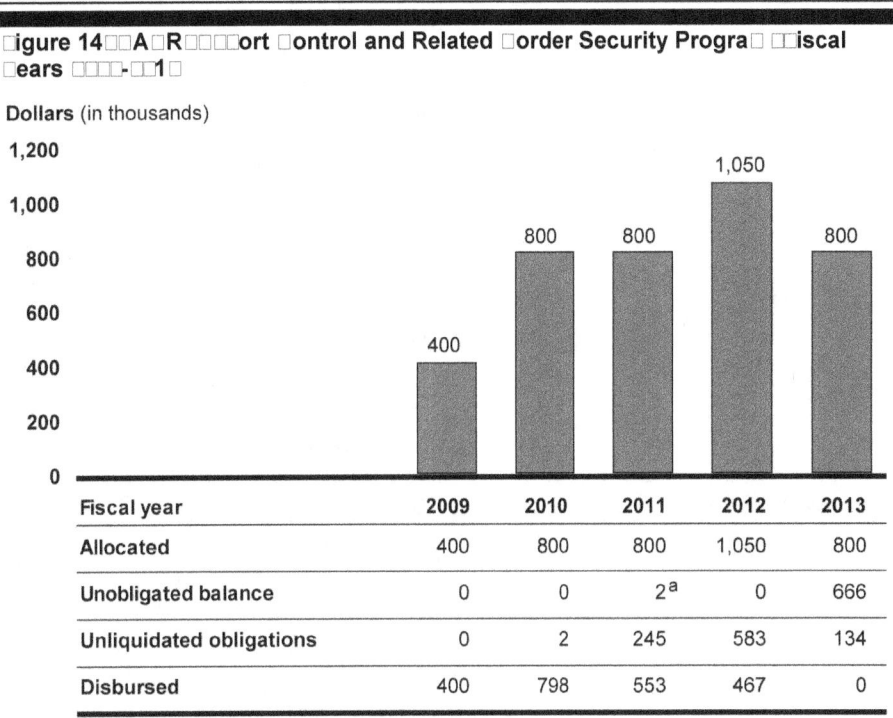

Dollars (in thousands)

Fiscal year	2009	2010	2011	2012	2013
Allocated	400	800	800	1,050	800
Unobligated balance	0	0	2[a]	0	666
Unliquidated obligations	0	2	245	583	134
Disbursed	400	798	553	467	0

NADR = Nonproliferation, Antiterrorism, Demining, and Related Programs

Source: GAO analysis of State data.

Notes:

NADR funding supports the Export Control and Related Border Security program, which is managed and implemented by State with some implementation by a broader set of agencies.

NADR Export Control and Related Border Security funds are generally available for obligation for 2 years. All NADR obligations continue to be available for expenditure for an additional 5 years after the end of their period of availability for obligation.

[a]According to State, unobligated balance in fiscal year 2011 is no longer available for obligation.

Figure 12: Section 1207 Authority Program Fiscal Years 2009-2013

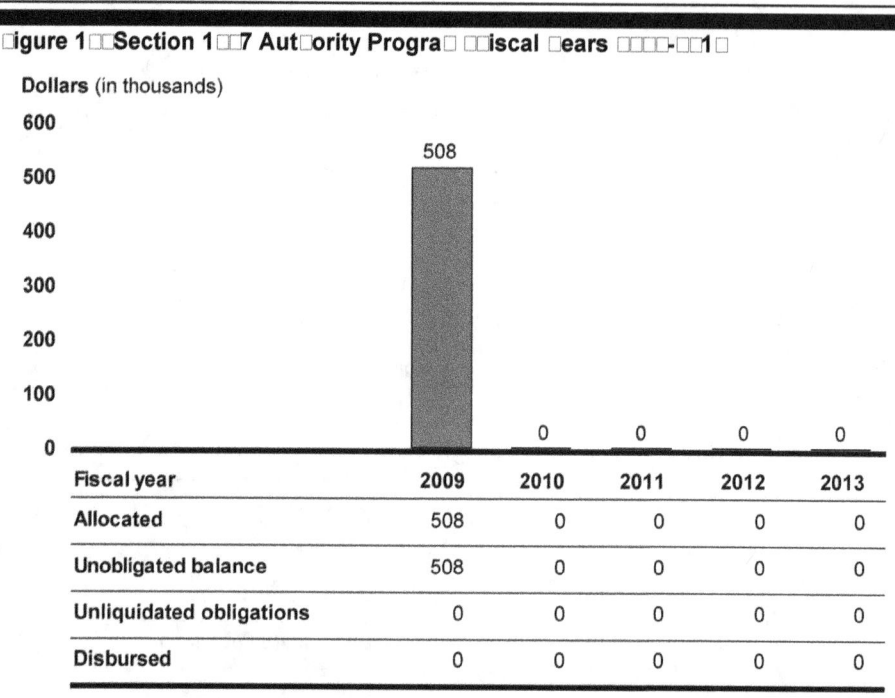

Dollars (in thousands)

Fiscal year	2009	2010	2011	2012	2013
Allocated	508	0	0	0	0
Unobligated balance	508	0	0	0	0
Unliquidated obligations	0	0	0	0	0
Disbursed	0	0	0	0	0

Source: GAO analysis of State data.

Notes: The authority for Section 1207 expired at the end of fiscal year 2010. Although funded through DOD, Section 1207 funds were transferred to the Department of State for management. When Section 1207 funds were transferred to State, they became "no year" money and remain available until expended.

Appendix IV: Comments from the Department of Defense

OFFICE OF THE SECRETARY OF DEFENSE

WASHINGTON, DC 20301

Mr. Charles Johnson, Jr.
Director, International Affairs and Trade
U.S. Government Accountability Office
441 G Street, NW
Washington, DC 20548

Dear Mr. Johnson:

This is the Department of Defense (DoD) response to the GAO Draft Report GAO-14-161, "Countering Overseas Threats: DoD and State Need to Address Gaps in Monitoring Security Equipment Transferred to Lebanon," dated January 27, 2014 (GAO Code 320975).

The Department is providing official written comments for inclusion in the report.

Sincerely,

Matthew Spence
Deputy Assistant Secretary
Middle East

Attachment
As Stated

**GAO DRAFT REPORT DATED JANUARY 27, 2014
GAO-14-161 (GAO CODE 320975)**

**"COUNTERING OVERSEAS THREATS: DOD AND STATE NEED TO ADDRESS
GAPS IN MONITORING SECURITY EQUIPMENT TRANSFERRED TO LEBANON"**

**DEPARTMENT OF DEFENSE COMMENTS
TO THE GAO RECOMMENDATION**

RECOMMENDATION 1: The GAO recommends that the Secretary of Defense take additional steps to ensure that Office of Defense Cooperation officials in Beirut use the checklists required during the physical security checks.

DoD RESPONSE: Concur. The Department of Defense has published policy guidance regarding the Golden Sentry End-Use Monitoring (EUM) program in the Security Assistance Management Manual (SAMM), Chapter 8, Section C8.4 for defense articles and services designated for Enhanced End-Use Monitoring (EEUM). This policy guidance provides that all Security Cooperation Organizations (SCOs), such as the Office of Defense Cooperation (ODC) in Beirut, use checklists available in the Security Cooperation Information Portal database to conduct EEUM checks (SAMM policy excerpt attached).

The ODC in Beirut has developed EUM Standard Operating Procedures (SOP) that require ODC officials to use the appropriate checklists when performing physical security and accountability checks of defense articles designated for EEUM (Paragraph 7.b.2 of the attached ODC EUM SOP). The ODC has implemented the procedures, and ODC officials are now using the checklists to perform the required EEUM checks. Additionally, to continue its excellent record of monitoring the Lebanese Armed Forces' compliance with the EUM program, the ODC is now maintaining the checklists for five years, as required by EUM policy in the SAMM, as a record of the EEUM checks performed.

Appendix V: Comments from the U.S. Department of State

United States Department of State
Comptroller
P.O. Box 150008
Charleston, SC 29415-5008

FEB 1 9 2014

Dr. Loren Yager
Managing Director
International Affairs and Trade
Government Accountability Office
441 G Street, N.W.
Washington, D.C. 20548-0001

Dear Dr. Yager:

We appreciate the opportunity to review your draft report, "Countering Overseas Threats: DOD and State Need to Address Gaps in Monitoring Security Equipment Transferred to Lebanon" GAO Job Code 320975.

The enclosed Department of State comments are provided for incorporation with this letter as an appendix to the final report.

If you have any questions concerning this response, please contact Josh Paul, Director, Bureau of Political-Military Affairs at (202) 647-7878.

Sincerely,

James L. Millette

cc: GAO – Charles Michael Johnson
       PM – Tom Kelly
       State/OIG – Norman Brown

STATE DEPARTMENT RESPONSE TO GAO REPORT

**COUNTERING OVERSEAS THREATS: DOD AND STATE NEED TO
ADDRESS GAPS IN MONITORING SECURITY EQUIPMENT
TRANSFERRED TO LEBANON (GAO 14-161)**

Thank you for the opportunity to comment on your draft report entitled
*"Countering overseas threats: DoD and State need to address gaps in monitoring
security equipment transferred to Lebanon"*

The Department of State agrees with the recommendation that it maintain
records of cables and emails that document each Blue Lantern end-use check. The
Department disagrees with the finding that it did not adequately do so with regard
to Lebanon, as asserted in the draft report. Maintaining such records has been, and
remains, the Department's general, long-standing practice. In the particular cases
cited by GAO, the Department did document key findings of the four inquiries in
the Blue Lantern database, as these cases were adjudicated together as a group
involving the same foreign consignee and Lebanese Security Forces.

The Department also notes that Blue Lantern checks are routinely conducted
on items authorized for export, but not yet exported. With respect to the records in
question, the GAO inaccurately refers to defense articles that were "exported" to
Lebanon. The GAO should have referred to defense articles that were
"authorized" for export to Lebanon, as several defense articles had not yet been
exported at the time of the Blue Lantern checks.

The Department agrees with the recommendation that all exports authorized
by the Bureau of International Narcotics and Law Enforcement Affairs should
receive, at a minimum, a standard level of end-use monitoring, that such standards
should be directed in writing, and that the Directorate of Defense Trade Controls
should be consulted when such transfers are made.

Appendix VI: GAO Contact and Staff Acknowledgments

GAO Contact	Charles Michael Johnson, Jr., 202-512-7331, or johnsoncm@gao.gov
Staff Acknowledgments	In addition to the contact named above, Jeff Phillips (Assistant Director), Claude Adrien, Jenna Beveridge, David Dayton, Justin Fisher, Julia Ann Roberts, and La Verne Tharpes made key contributions to this report. Martin de Alteriis, Jeff Isaacs, Grace Lui, and Etana Finkler provided additional technical assistance.

GAO's Mission	The Government Accountability Office, the audit, evaluation, and investigative arm of Congress, exists to support Congress in meeting its constitutional responsibilities and to help improve the performance and accountability of the federal government for the American people. GAO examines the use of public funds; evaluates federal programs and policies; and provides analyses, recommendations, and other assistance to help Congress make informed oversight, policy, and funding decisions. GAO's commitment to good government is reflected in its core values of accountability, integrity, and reliability.
Obtaining Copies of GAO Reports and Testimony	The fastest and easiest way to obtain copies of GAO documents at no cost is through GAO's website (http://www.gao.gov). Each weekday afternoon, GAO posts on its website newly released reports, testimony, and correspondence. To have GAO e-mail you a list of newly posted products, go to http://www.gao.gov and select "E-mail Updates."
Order by Phone	The price of each GAO publication reflects GAO's actual cost of production and distribution and depends on the number of pages in the publication and whether the publication is printed in color or black and white. Pricing and ordering information is posted on GAO's website, http://www.gao.gov/ordering.htm.
	Place orders by calling (202) 512-6000, toll free (866) 801-7077, or TDD (202) 512-2537.
	Orders may be paid for using American Express, Discover Card, MasterCard, Visa, check, or money order. Call for additional information.
Connect with GAO	Connect with GAO on Facebook, Flickr, Twitter, and YouTube. Subscribe to our RSS Feeds or E-mail Updates. Listen to our Podcasts. Visit GAO on the web at www.gao.gov.
To Report Fraud, Waste, and Abuse in Federal Programs	Contact: Website: http://www.gao.gov/fraudnet/fraudnet.htm E-mail: fraudnet@gao.gov Automated answering system: (800) 424-5454 or (202) 512-7470
Congressional Relations	Katherine Siggerud, Managing Director, siggerudk@gao.gov, (202) 512-4400, U.S. Government Accountability Office, 441 G Street NW, Room 7125, Washington, DC 20548
Public Affairs	Chuck Young, Managing Director, youngc1@gao.gov, (202) 512-4800 U.S. Government Accountability Office, 441 G Street NW, Room 7149 Washington, DC 20548

www.ingramcontent.com/pod-product-compliance
Lightning Source LLC
Chambersburg PA
CBHW080546290526
45790CB00006B/2570